The MACAT Library

世界思想宝库钥匙丛书

解析迈克尔·E.波特

《竞争战略：
分析产业和竞争对手的技术》

AN ANALYSIS OF

MICHAEL E. PORTER'S

COMPETITIVE STRATEGY:

Techniques for Analyzing Industries
and Competitors

Pádraig Belton ◎ 著

陶庆 ◎ 译

上海外语教育出版社
外教社 SHANGHAI FOREIGN LANGUAGE EDUCATION PRESS

MACAT

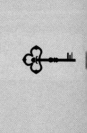

目　录

CONTENTS

引言

要 点

- 迈克尔·E. 波特是美国哈佛大学商学院教授。他 1947 年出生于美国密歇根州，作为其父的随军家属，他成长的足迹遍及世界各地。

- 在 1980 年出版的《竞争战略》中，波特把行业中的竞争*因素分为五类，即供应商*（供应企业所需原料的商户）、买方（客户）、替代产品*（简而言之，就是产品或服务的廉价替代品）、潜在入市者（可能进入某一特定市场的新竞争者）和业内竞争对手。

- 过去 30 年中，波特的《竞争战略》不仅塑造了企业领导的思维方式，而且吸引了渴望了解成功企业运营模式的学者和大众。

迈克尔·E. 波特其人

《竞争战略：分析产业和竞争对手的技术》（1980）的作者迈克尔·E. 波特 1947 年出生于美国密歇根州的安娜堡。他父亲是职业军人，迈克尔成长过程中跟随其父在不同国家居住。他在普林斯顿大学主修航空航天和机械工程专业，1969 年以全班第一名的成绩毕业。然后赴哈佛大学深造，1971 年以优异成绩获得哈佛商学院工商管理硕士学位，并于 1973 年获得商业经济学博士学位。

波特的主要研究领域为竞争战略*，即企业或机构负责人运用何种方法可以提高利润或使自己的企业或机构超越对手，以及如何提升竞争力。他对该领域的研究兴趣源于他小时候参加体育活动的经历。中学期间他曾是本州最佳棒球和橄榄球运动员之一；大学期间他是全美最佳大学生高尔夫球选手之一。[1]

获得博士学位后，波特在哈佛商学院任教，继续从事学术研究。1980 年，他出版了《竞争战略》第一版。该书很快成为极具影响力的商业书籍，并成为全球畅销书。截至 2016 年，该书被译成 19 种语言，重印 63 次。哈佛商学院以及几乎全球所有商学院都把该书列为核心教材。

2001 年起，波特担任哈佛商学院战略与竞争力研究所主任。他已成为管理和经济学领域引用率最高的学者之一。[2]

他的后续作品又将《竞争战略》中的观点进一步拓展，从国家层面审视竞争力并关注竞争与社会的关系。

波特还担任了美国各级官员、多国政府和大量企业的顾问，帮助他们将《竞争战略》中的理念付诸实施。作为体育爱好者，他还依据竞争战略为波士顿红袜棒球队出谋划策。虽然他参与创建的咨询公司摩立特集团于 2012 年破产，但作为咨询顾问，他的事业总体还算成功。他现在定居马萨诸塞州的布鲁克莱恩。

《竞争战略》的主要内容

《竞争战略》为企业提供了一种卓有成效的思维框架，帮助他们分析行业中的竞争状况。这一框架以波特 1979 年在《哈佛商业评论》上发表的一篇文章为基础拓展而成。[3]

波特在《竞争战略》的第一节描述了影响竞争的五大关键因素（"五力"）*：供应商、买方、替代产品、潜在入市者和业内竞争对手。这一框架是了解竞争环境的有力工具。[4] 当然，他的主要目的在于帮助企业找到最有效的制胜之道。

在波特看来，若想克敌制胜，要么提高效率，降低成本；要么另辟蹊径，与众不同，提升质量或用户体验：两者必居其一，别无他途。

波特认为，对企业业绩产生影响的不仅仅是竞争对手，环境因素同样至关重要。买方、卖方、尚未入行的公司（今后也许会进入）、其他产品等都很重要。这种视角可谓标新立异，同当时多数商业领域学者公认的观点截然不同。先前管理领域的专家主要关注如何扩大市场份额等问题，而波特认为这些并非关键所在。

航空业便是波特理论的有力佐证。爱尔兰瑞安航空公司*定位为以低价取胜，侧重成本领先*，一切业务围绕减少间接费用这一中心，从而降低票价。与此相反，企业也可以选择提供竞争对手无法提供的服务或技术创新，从而提升价格。以新加坡航空公司为例，它是首家为经济舱客户提供单独电视屏幕的航空公司。推而广之，如果一家公司能够找到适合自身运营的小众市场，如提供私人飞机服务，那么同样会取得成功。

通过低价产品或差异化产品开展竞争的创意并不是波特发明的，但他提出了全新的视角和系统的方法，使这一理论框架能便捷地应用于各个行业。他借鉴了比较优势*这一19世纪提出的经济学概念，即国家也好，公司也罢，都应该专注于自己能以最低成本、最高效率生产的产品。他用全新且易懂的方法将这些观念运用于现代企业，效果极佳。

《竞争战略》分析了如何在不同行业中运用这一理论框架。在波特看来，行业中存在不同的层次，其中不同的公司针对不同的市场开展业务（以服装行业为例，既有低价的大众市场，也有高价的精品市场）。他还分析了企业在新兴市场、成熟市场、衰退市场中分别应该采取哪些不同的策略。比方说，虽然我们认为印刷行业处于衰退之中，但对其中的高端产品和服务仍有市场需求，譬如豪华工艺装订和凸版印刷（一种用活动铅字排版的传统印刷技艺）。

波特的研究激励了其他学者深入分析竞争的特点。在《竞争战略》的基础之上，他又于1985年出版了《竞争优势：如何创造并保持骄人业绩》，书中提出了价值链*这一新概念，用于审视企业生产和服务的各个环节。

波特的高明之处在于用五种关键因素概括了商业竞争的各种形态，因此吸引了来自经济学界、企业高管和社会大众的众多读者。

《竞争战略》的学术价值

自从1980年面世以来，《竞争战略》始终被视为一部重要作品。全球各地的商学院都将它作为培养商界领袖了解竞争市场的教材。哈佛商学院以该书内容为基础，为财富500强*（由美国《财富》杂志评选的美国最大的500家公司）新任CEO开设培训课程。该书被视为过去40年中在商界和管理学界影响力最大的书籍之一。[5]

该书提出的"五力"分析法有助于企业高管经营业务时设立明确的战略目标，做到知己知彼，洞悉行业发展趋势。

波特的工具能够帮助业界人士提前谋划，犹如下棋时比对手多想几步，而不是一味关注短期运营问题。

除了提供有关竞争分析的理论框架，《竞争战略》还为企业提供具体指导。举例而言，定位为低成本战略的公司可以从波特理论中的五个竞争因素中得到启发，免遭任一因素会带来的不利影响。既不属于低成本策略，又不属于差异化策略的公司可以赚取溢价，但也容易陷入不上不下的困境，需要长时间努力方能摆脱。波特研究了这一现象，称之为"中区陷阱问题"*。

《竞争战略》获奖无数，其中包括管理科学院颁发的管理思想杰出贡献奖。目前有四个以波特名字命名的奖项，用于奖励在各自领域出色运用波特原理的公司。这四个奖项分别设在日本（2001）、印度（2012）、韩国（2014）以及更加宏观层面的医疗卫生行业（2014）。[6]

　　对于希望了解公司应该如何制定战略，从而获得竞争优势的读者来说，几十年前出版的《竞争战略》仍然属于必读书目。多伦多大学罗特曼商学院院长罗杰·马丁*评价道，"如果有人谈及如何获得可持续竞争优势，那他必定是运用了从波特的《竞争战略》一书中衍生的商业概念。"[7]

---

1. 沃尔特·基希勒三世：《战略简史：引领企业竞争的思想进化论》，马萨诸塞州坎布里奇：哈佛商业出版社，2010 年。

2. 琼·玛格雷塔：《竞争战略论：一本书读懂迈克尔·波特》，马萨诸塞州坎布里奇：哈佛商业评论出版社，2011 年。

3. 迈克尔·E. 波特："竞争因素如何塑造战略"，《哈佛商业评论》第 57 卷，1979 年第 2 期，第 86—93 页。

4. 迈克尔·E. 波特：《竞争战略：分析产业和竞争对手的技术》（第二版），纽约：自由出版社，1998 年。

5. 阿瑟·贝德安和丹尼尔·雷恩："20 世纪最具影响力的管理书籍"，《组织活力》第 29 卷，2001 年第 3 期，第 221—225 页。

6. 波特奖："简介"，登录日期 2016 年 1 月 29 日，http://www.porterprize.org/english/about/。

7. 杰夫·科尔文："坚定不移的迈克尔·波特"，《财富》，2012 年 10 月 15 日，登录日期 2016 年 1 月 29 日，http://fortune.com/2012/10/15/theres-no-quit-in-michael-porter/。

第一部分：学术渊源

1 作者生平与历史背景

要点 🗝

- 对于商业领域中的战略（即如何制定计划，实现目标）和竞争，《竞争战略》提出了全新的思考方式。

- 波特儿时对竞技体育的兴趣激发了他研究如何运用战略参与竞争。

- 《竞争战略》发表后，几乎所有的商学院毕业生都会学习书中提出的原理，使该书在商业界产生了巨大影响。

为何要读这部著作？

迈克尔·E.波特的《竞争战略：分析产业和竞争对手的技术》（1980）是商业管理和战略领域影响力最大的作品之一。在曾任著名商业期刊《哈佛商业评论》编辑的琼·玛格雷塔*看来，波特是"经济学和商业领域作品引用率最高的学者。同时，他的理念也广泛被世界各地政府和企业领导付诸实践。他的理论框架已经成为战略领域的基石。"[1]

《竞争战略》介绍了若干重要概念，特别是五大要素（"五力"），即供应商（供应企业所需原料的商户）、买方（客户）、替代方（产品或服务的廉价替代品）、潜在入市者（可能进入某一特定市场的新竞争者）和行业内的竞争对手。其他核心概念包括竞争优势*（帮助企业超越竞争对手的元素）、价值链*（企业生产产品和提供服务所涉及的所有活动）、行业结构*（商业环境的性质）和差异化*（生产与众不同的产品）。

如今这些概念被广泛应用，但很多场合下由于理解不够准确或不够完整，这些概念被曲解了。[2] 要真正理解《竞争战略》的精髓并付诸实践，我们必须了解并避免常见的错误观念。

有一种认识误区，即竞争的目的是做到最好；而波特认为，竞争的实质在于做到与众不同。许多人误以为竞争就是对手之间你死我活的争斗，其实，企业竞争的核心在于获取利润。许多人以为战略针对的是所有客户，其实战略的实施是为了有选择地取悦部分客户。[3] 在波特看来，成功的战略还在于故意使某些客户感到不悦。

> "一个企业所处竞争环境的性质与其盈亏表现息息相关。"
> —— 迈克尔·E. 波特：《竞争战略：分析产业和竞争对手的技术》

作者生平

波特 1947 年出生于密歇根州的一个军人家庭，幼时曾在不同国家居住，受到各种文化熏陶。回美国读中学和大学时，他在棒球、橄榄球和高尔夫球等竞技体育项目中表现十分出色，这也增加了他研究竞争和战略的兴趣。

波特的学术生涯始于工程领域，他 1969 年毕业于普林斯顿大学工程专业，然后他将自己的技术与数学技能运用于商业和经济学。本科毕业后，他旋即就读于哈佛商学院，并获得工商管理硕士学位（MBA）。然后他继续深造，于 1973 年获得商业经济学博士学位。

波特以其在竞争力和战略领域的作品著称于世，他把这些作品所包含的思想整合进了他于 1980 年出版的《竞争战略》一书中。他在此前一年发表于《哈佛商业评论》的一篇学术论文中就开始了对书中提及观点的研究，[4]并在后续出版的作品（特别是《竞争优势：如何创造并保持骄人业绩》（1985））中拓展了《竞争战略》中的观点。他总共出版了 19 本著作，被公认为现代战略研究之父。[5]他目前担任哈佛大学 24 个最高教授职位之一，威廉·劳伦斯主教大学讲席教授。

2000 年，哈佛大学在哈佛商学院成立了战略与竞争力研究所。哈佛商学院的网站上描述其使命为"深入开展由波特开创的研究并将其成果传播给全球各地的学者和从业人员"。[6]该研究所重点研究竞争及其对公司战略的影响，国家、地区、城市等大型实体的竞争力，以及竞争与社会的关系。

创作背景

波特的早期工作主要是运用经济学理论更完整地理解企业如何进行竞争决策，以及某一行业竞争的相互作用。《竞争战略》中两个最重要的主题是行业结构（从企业、客户、产品等角度分析市场构成）和战略定位 *（用以帮助企业在市场中找到最有利的位置）。再加上他后来提出的价值链（企业向市场推出产品过程中涉及的所有环节），这些构成了波特理论的核心。

20 世纪 80 年代的美国，既经历着经济扩张，又感受到了东亚（尤其是日本）企业崛起所带来的不安全感。《竞争战略》给美国企业提供了如何规划与日本企业展开竞争的理论框架。

出版了《竞争战略》以后，波特的研究重点转向更大规模的经济发展和竞争力，即利用微观经济学 *（研究小规模经济，如某单一公司的决策等）因素来研究不同地区和国家的经济发展。他提出了集群 * 的概念并创建了集群映射项目 *，研究美国不同地区的相关商业集群。他还参与开创了经济地理学研究 *，即研究如何在供应商、工作人员和相关企业之间进行最佳匹配，以降低运输成本，减少运输距离，从而使某些行业在部分地区的发展快于其他地区。

波特还将《竞争战略》中的理念运用到医疗卫生和企业社会责任等领域。他后来的作品，尤其是和商业战略家马克·克莱默 * 合作于 2011 年发表的文章《创造共享价值》，[7] 使企业改变了对社会责任 * 的认知。波特认为企业社会责任并非慈善工作（捐钱给别人），而是通过在各地设置商业项目和创建企业来帮助贫困群体，从而创造社会价值。

同样闻名于世的还有"波特假说" *。该假说认为，严格的环境标准能够激励企业创新和提高效率，从而提高企业利润，提升国家竞争力。这一假说引发了环境经济学领域数百篇研究论文的发表。[8]

诚如《财富》杂志一位资深编辑所言："波特对企业高管、各国政府产生的影响比世界上任何一位商学院教授都大。"[9]

---

1. 琼·玛格雷塔：《竞争战略论：一本书读懂迈克尔·波特》，马萨诸塞州坎布里奇：哈佛商业评论出版社，2011 年。

2. 见玛格雷塔：《一本书读懂迈克尔·波特》，第 121—140 页。

3. 玛格雷塔：《一本书读懂迈克尔·波特》，第 111 页。

4. 迈克尔·E.波特："竞争因素如何塑造战略"，《哈佛商业评论》第 57 卷，1979 年第 2 期，第 86—93 页。

5. 安东尼奥·涅托·罗德里格斯：《专注的组织：聚焦重要举措如何快速提升战略执行力》，佛蒙特州伯灵顿：阿什盖特出版社，第 202 页。

6. 哈佛大学策略与竞争力研究所："主页"，登录日期 2016 年 1 月 29 日，http://www.isc.hbs.edu/。

7. 迈克尔·E. 波特和马克·R.克莱默："创造共享价值"，《哈佛商业评论》，2011年，第 63—70 页。

8. 谷歌学术："波特假说"，登录日期 2016 年 1 月 29 日，https://scholar.google.com/scholar?hl=en&q=%22Porter+Hypothesis%22&btnG=&as_sdt=1%2C9&as_sdtp=。

9. 杰夫·科尔文："坚定不移的迈克尔·波特"，《财富》，2012 年 10 月 15 日，登录日期 2016 年 1 月 29 日，http://fortune.com/2012/10/15/theres-no-quit-in-michael-porter/。

2 学术背景

要点 🔑

- 战略一词始于军事行动和政府部门，二战*（1939—1945）后开始成为商界用语。
- 哈佛商学院的肯尼斯·安德鲁斯*等学者把这一概念移植到商业语境，用于教授商科学生。
- 《竞争战略》写于20世纪末，当时出现了大量管理专家，他们致力于研究企业成功经营所面临的诸多挑战。

著作语境

在《竞争战略：分析产业和竞争对手的技术》中，迈克尔·E.波特把战略*定义为"关于企业如何开展竞争，如何设定目标，以及实现目标所需政策的总体规划"。[1]波特认为，"战略就是企业为之奋斗的目标和实现目标之方式的综合体。"[2]

波特关于商业竞争的一个核心观点是，企业应该专注于特定市场，而不是面对整个市场和所有客户。这一观点可以追溯到19世纪经济学家大卫·李嘉图*提出的比较优势*的思想。根据李嘉图的理论，每个国家都应该尽可能地在其最具竞争优势的细分领域从事生产。比如说，石油输出国组织*（OPEC）成员国应该专注于生产原油，加拿大应该专注于生产枫糖浆等特色产品。

假设A产品是能以最低边际成本*生产的产品，那么生产任何A产品以外的其他产品（B产品）即意味着必须多支出因生产B产品而产生的机会成本*，而如果只生产A产品就不会出现这一机会成本。"边际成本"是指多生产一件产品的额外成本。"机会成本"是指实际产品之最佳替代品的价值。

如果一个能够以最低边际成本生产 A 产品的国家将其资源用于生产更多的 A 产品,那么就可以将多余的 A 产品卖出,然后从能够以最高效率生产 B 产品的国家购入 B 产品。比如说,冰岛的渔业非常发达。它可以大量出口鳕鱼,用所得收入购买许多自己无法高效率生产的产品,例如香蕉。这是明智之举。如果冰岛不这样做,而是减少渔业投入,投资人力物力建造昂贵的暖房来种植香蕉,那么结果将是可供出售的鳕鱼减少,吃到的香蕉也更少,得不偿失。

李嘉图关于比较优势的论断就是现今各国普遍采纳的自由贸易原则的理论基础:每个国家都集中资源生产自己最擅长的产品,将多余部分出售给其他国家,用这笔收入来购买自己不擅长生产的产品,这样能买到的其他产品必定比自己生产得到的更多。

在《竞争战略》中,波特指出各个公司都应该集中精力关注某一特定领域,如开采资源(开挖矿产或开采原油等)、制造某种产品或提供某种服务。

> "许多有关企业竞争的书籍只关注个案,或只以特定情况而非普适的竞争战略为依据开展分析,所以很快就被人们淡忘了。"
>
> —— 迈克尔·E. 波特:《竞争战略:分析产业和竞争对手的技术》

学科概览

"战略"一词可能自城邦诞生之日起就出现了。城邦统治者运用战略（军事计划）和战术（军事举措）战胜对手。该词出自希腊语 Stratēgia，意思是"为将之道"。Stratēgos 是"将军"的意思，是公元前 4 世纪马其顿军事领袖和征服者亚历山大大帝 * 及其父亲腓力二世 * 的头衔。随着时间的推移，战略领域的研究日渐丰富，包含了军事战略、商业战略以及其他一切涉及竞争的领域。

然而，战略研究从军事领域转向商业领域则是二战后的事情。商业战略家肯尼斯·安德鲁斯在其中发挥了关键作用。他凭借对美国著名作家马克·吐温 * 的研究获得博士学位，然后在二战期间从军参战，并于 1946 年成为哈佛商学院的教师。1950 年，他和几个同事开始修订哈佛商学院的商业政策课程。两年后，他们选择使用公司战略这一概念作为该课程的组织原则。

安德鲁斯开始从企业高管的角度撰写案例分析（对真实事例的研究分析），研究涉及如何识别威胁和机遇、如何理解公司的价值等一系列公司面临的问题和挑战。这一课程催生了两本重要教材：《经营策略：内容与案例》（1965）和《公司战略的概念》（1971）。[3]

根据安德鲁斯的早期定义，战略是有针对性的行为，即管理层有意识地制定和实施的策略。他认为战略必须符合道德标准，同时必须符合企业高管的价值观。

加拿大学者亨利·明茨伯格 * 也是一位商业战略专家，他提出了另一种观点。在他看来，安德鲁斯的理论过于关注顶层（即企业高管），不够民主。他强调了"应急战略" * 的重要性，他所称的"应急战略"就是在组织的任一层级以非正式形式出现的战略。这是对企业高管精心思考后决定或认可的战略的调整和补充。

学术渊源

《竞争战略》中不仅有波特的思想，还包括了其他同事的贡献。1970年加盟哈佛商学院的商业历史学家阿尔弗雷德·D.钱德勒*因其著作《看得见的手：美国企业的管理革命》于1977年获得普利策奖（一个著名的文学奖项）。[4]钱德勒的著作就是"管理革命"*的组成部分，该书分析了管理者在大型企业的组织和运营中的重要性。

钱德勒早先还写了《战略与结构：美国工商企业成长的若干篇章》（1962），该书分析了美国大企业的战略是如何决定其架构的。[5]钱德勒总结道，"企业架构服从于企业战略。"[6]

有些学者马上提出不同观点，认为企业战略服从于企业架构。比如，多部门的结构（指公司被分割成独立性很强的不同部门）促使企业采纳混合多元化战略*，[7]即鼓励多样化经营，通过增加新产品或服务种类进入不同于现有业务的领域。

把《竞争战略》和20世纪其他管理学巨著做一比较很有意义。影响力最大的仍属早期管理学专家弗雷德里克·温斯洛·泰勒*的《科学管理原理》（1911）。[8]泰勒认为企业效率最高的做法是把工作任务标准化，这样能在最短时间内完成任务。这本书是管理学的开山之作。

紧随其后的是研究商业的学者切斯特·伯纳德*的《经理人员的职能》（1938）。[9]这是首批从社会和心理的角度（即研究头脑在行为中的作用）考察领导力的专著之一。赫伯特·西蒙*给自己的1947年专著取名《管理行为：管理组织决策过程的研究》，非常妥帖。该书至今仍是社会科学领域中引用率最高的管理学著作之一。[10]

1967 年，管理学专家保罗·劳伦斯 * 和杰伊·洛希 * 出版了颇具影响力的《组织与环境》[11]，对先前的观点提出了质疑。他们问道：是否存在一种不受行业、市场和整体商业环境等具体情况制约的最佳组织方式？劳伦斯和洛奇认为不存在这样的模式，相反，他们提出了权变理论 *。这一理论认为，理想的领导模式应该随具体任务和环境的不同而变化。

在波特加入哈佛商学院以前，该商学院已在商业战略领域拥有成熟的研究传统，而波特的《竞争战略》吸收了这些成果。不过，先前的著作主要关注的是伦理和效率，而波特把对战略的研讨重点转向市场中不同公司之间的冲突。

1. 迈克尔·E. 波特：《竞争战略：分析产业和竞争对手的技术》（第二版），纽约：自由出版社，1998 年，第 xxiv 页。

2. 波特：《竞争战略》，第 xxiv 页。

3. 菲利普·勒恩德等：《经营策略：内容与案例》，伊利诺伊州霍姆伍德：欧文出版社，1969 年；肯尼斯·R. 安德鲁斯：《公司战略的概念》，伊利诺伊州霍姆伍德：欧文出版社，1994 年。

4. 阿尔弗雷德·钱德勒：《看得见的手：美国企业的管理革命》，马萨诸塞州坎布里奇：哈佛大学贝尔纳普出版社，1977 年。

5. 阿尔弗雷德·钱德勒：《战略与结构：美国工商企业成长的若干篇章》，马萨诸塞州坎布里奇：麻省理工学院出版社，1962 年。

6. 钱德勒：《战略与结构》，第 14 页。

7. 大卫·霍尔和莫里斯·萨亚斯："战略紧随结构"，《战略管理》第 1 卷，1980 年第 2 期，第 149—163 页。

8. 弗雷德里克·温斯洛·泰勒：《科学管理原理》，纽约：哈珀兄弟出版社，1911 年。

9. 切斯特·巴纳德：《经理人员的职能》，马萨诸塞州坎布里奇：哈佛大学出版社，1938年。

10. 赫伯特·西蒙：《管理行为：管理组织决策过程的研究》，纽约：麦克米伦出版社，1947年。

11. 保罗·劳伦斯和杰伊·洛希：《组织与环境》，马萨诸塞州波士顿：哈佛商学院研究部，1967年。

3 主导命题

要点 🗝

- 整个 20 世纪 50 年代中期，所有企业都专注于通过提高产量来增加利润。随着客户选择的增加，波特提出应关注如何提高某一特定市场的客户满意度。

- 波特于 20 世纪 70 年代提出的理论吸收了当时几种各不相同的主流商业战略模型的研究成果。

- 波特发现所有的主流模型都存在缺陷，他最后从经济学家乔·贝恩 * 的模型中得到了重要启发。乔·贝恩的结构—行为—绩效模型 * 主要分析市场结构如何影响商业绩效。

核心问题

在《竞争战略：分析产业和竞争对手的技术》中，迈克尔·E. 波特提出的问题是：企业如何最有效地挑选有利可图的行业开展竞争？找到合适的行业后，采取何种战略可以使自己最有效地与对手竞争？

他提出了问题：企业如何在本行业内就自身竞争优势 *（能够使自己比对手表现更出色的能力）所涉及的范围和类别作出重要选择？此前的研究认为，商业战略的目标应该是尽可能多销售产品。[1]波特对这一结论并不满意。而且，这并不符合对利润和效率最高的公司所开展的实证研究的结果。

在 20 世纪 50 年代中期，以生产为导向 * 的战略在行业中占主导地位。该观点假定，企业如能创造出高技术附加值且经久耐用的产品，就能得到利润回报。

哈佛商学院教授西奥多·莱维特*1960年在《哈佛商业评论》发表了一篇名为《营销短视》*的重要文章，帮助人们改变以生产为导向的模型。他建议企业转为客户导向，重视满足客户需求，而不是先设计出一款优质产品，然后再考虑如何销售。[2]

这方面有一个经典例子。福特汽车的创始人亨利·福特*曾戏言，客户可以选择任何颜色的黑色T型车（第一款大批量生产的、价格相对低廉的轿车）。[3]当时，消费品短缺，而且在20世纪20到30年代经济大萧条*（灾难性的经济衰退）和二战*（1939—1945）期间，这一情况尤为严重。这意味着企业只要生产出性能优越的产品就能找到市场。

莱维特提出的以客户为中心的模型看来更适合经济处于发展阶段、消费品供给日益增长的状况。当然，这一模型要求企业领导掌握一系列新工具用于战略决策，这些工具能帮助他们考虑诸如竞争对手的产品和客户面临的多种选择等比较宏观的问题。波特在《竞争战略》中讨论的就是这些工具。

> "制定竞争战略的实质在于将企业置于其生存环境之中……生存环境中最重要的就是企业所处的行业。某一行业的竞争强度并非偶然因素或坏运气所导致。一切竞争都源于深层的经济结构，而非只涉及当前竞争对手的行为。"
>
> —— 迈克尔·E.波特：《竞争战略：分析产业和竞争对手的技术》

参与者

对这一领域做出重大贡献的一位学者是加州斯坦福大学斯坦

福国际研究所*的阿尔伯特·汉弗莱*。他在20世纪60到70年代推广了SWOT分析法*，用以帮助企业针对竞争对手分析自身的优势、劣势、机遇和威胁。汉弗莱认为，如果一个企业所拥有的资源和具备的能力同其所处的外部环境中的机遇相匹配，那么就实现了战略契合*，即在市场中找到了合适的定位。

另一位重要学者是布鲁斯·亨德森*，管理咨询业巨头波士顿咨询集团*的创始人。他从1968年开始收集被专家称为"经验曲线"*的数据，用于战略研究。该曲线表明，一件事被重复的次数越多，做起来就越容易，效率也就越高。最早于1936年在俄亥俄州代顿的莱特-帕特森空军基地*做的测试发现，机务工作量翻倍以后，单位工作时间缩短10%到15%；在其他行业，这一数据可高达30%。

亨德森指出，降低运营成本能够给企业带来显著的竞争优势。因此，企业应该专注于扩大市场份额*（某一企业在市场中所占有的百分比），这样能够充分利用经验曲线。在亨德森看来，同一产品生产越多，员工的生产经验就越丰富，这样就能获得超越竞争对手的优势。

第三位关键人物是乔·贝恩，一位行业组织经济学*的重要学者。贝恩关注的重点不是企业或经济的整体运营状况，而是某一特定行业。在分析了某一行业的准入壁垒等问题后，他提出了被称为"结构—行为—绩效"的研究范式。这种范式注重从"竞争环境"、客户构成、产品等角度分析市场结构如何影响企业绩效。[4]

第四位重要学者和贝恩一样对波特产生过重要影响，他就是波特在哈佛商学院的同事阿尔弗雷德·D.钱德勒。在波特的《竞争战略》出版前三年，钱德勒的著作《看得见的手：美国企业的管理革命》获得了普利策奖。

当时的论战

在《竞争战略》出版以前，商业战略方面的主流观点来自亨德森的理论，即应鼓励公司尽可能扩大市场份额以便充分利用经验曲线带来的优势。

后来这一理论受到了挑战。20 世纪 60 年代后期，美国商界巨头通用电气公司 * 的市场营销分析师西德尼·舍福勒 * 开展了一个大规模研究项目——战略与绩效分析（PIMS）*。该项目采集了 1970 年至 1983 年期间 200 家公司中 2 600 个业务部门的观测数据，结果同亨德森的理论大相径庭：获得高额利润的不仅有市场份额很大的公司，也有市场份额很小的公司；市场份额不大不小的公司却是利润率最小的公司，这就是中区陷阱问题。[5] 波特还发现亨德森的 SWOT 分析法不够深入彻底，他转而研究乔·贝恩的理论，希望从中得到借鉴。

贝恩的结构—行为—绩效模型（波特的五力模型即以此为基础）探讨市场结构和行业绩效之间的关系。具体而言，该模型尤其关注一个行业内的企业行为与周边市场结构之间的关联，周边市场结构包括新企业进入的准入障碍、不同公司的产品差异、特定地区或客户群体中供需集中度等因素。

与此同时，钱德勒的《看得见的手：美国企业的管理革命》使公众广泛关注经营团队在复杂的现代企业组织管理中的重要性。[6] 但钱德勒的作品侧重的是经济学历史，而非商业战略。他在公众（包括波特）头脑中强调的是向专职商业管理人员提供其职业所需的专业技能。

1. 《经济学人》期刊编辑:"经验曲线",《经济学人》,2009 年 9 月 14 日,登录日期 2016 年 2 月 8 日,http://www.economist.com/node/14298944。

2. 西奥多·莱维特:"营销短视",《哈佛商业评论》,1960 年,第 45—60 页。

3. 亨利·福特和塞缪尔·克劳瑟:《我的生活与工作》,纽约州花园城:双日出版社,1923 年,第 72 页。

4. 乔·S. 贝恩:《产业组织》,纽约:约翰·威利父子出版社,1959 年。

5. 迈克尔·E. 波特:《竞争战略:分析产业和竞争对手的技术》(第二版),纽约:自由出版社,1998 年,第 42 页。

6. 阿尔弗雷德·钱德勒:《看得见的手:美国企业的管理革命》,马萨诸塞州坎布里奇:哈佛大学贝尔纳普出版社,1977 年。

4 作者贡献

要点 ⚰━

- 波特在《竞争战略》中提供了一种模型，用以分析某一行业中的竞争因素以及这些因素如何影响企业在这一行业中的盈利能力。

- 波特的五力模型包含了三种"横向"因素（现有竞争对手、新入市者和替代产品的威胁）和两种"纵向"因素（一方面是供应商的议价能力，另一方面是客户的议价能力）。

- 其他可供企业使用的战略规划工具还包括布鲁斯·亨德森*略显过时的增长率—占有率矩阵*，其关注重点是市场份额；还有包含政治、经济、社会和技术因素的 PEST 分析法*，这一方法如今常常和波特的五力模型一同被提起。

作者目标

在《竞争战略：分析产业和竞争对手的技术》中，迈克尔·E. 波特试图运用最新研究成果对影响企业竞争力的所有因素进行整体分析。正如波特所言，"某一行业的竞争涉及的远远不止现有企业。客户、供应商、替代产品、潜在入市者都可视为企业的竞争对手。随着具体情况变化，它们的重要程度也相应变化。"[1]

通过这一理论框架，企业经理和战略分析师可以了解各个因素的情况，并在此基础上做出进入哪一个市场、如何开展竞争的最佳决策。

《竞争战略》出版于 1980 年。波特自 1973 年获得商业经济学博士学位以后一直在哈佛商学院任教。他的思想深受就读时选修的行业组织经济学（探究企业和市场的架构）课程的影响，该课程旨在设计模型，用以分析竞争因素如何影响行业以及在不同环境下行业的盈利能力如何变化。

20世纪六七十年代，哈佛商学院的研究者如肯尼斯·安德鲁斯和阿尔弗雷德·D.钱德勒等一直在寻找企业盈利能力的驱动因素。这些研究使包括他们在内的许多学者对战略和高管角色等问题特别感兴趣。

但是，经理们用于分析战略问题的两大方法，SWOT分析法（优势、劣势、机遇和威胁）和经验曲线（即重复某项任务的次数越多，完成该任务所需的单位工作时间就越少）在波特看来都有缺陷。虽然SWOT分析法现在仍被广泛使用，但它并没有得到深入研究，也没有严格的理论基础。经验曲线则无法解释为什么市场份额较小的企业也能达到和市场份额较大的企业相同的盈利能力。

> "这（五种基本竞争）因素的综合作用决定了行业最终的盈利潜力，即资本投资的长期回报。并非所有的行业都有相同的潜力。"
>
> —— 迈克尔·E.波特：《竞争战略：分析产业和竞争对手的技术》

研究方法

波特的五力模型通过分析一个行业中影响企业盈利能力的因素对该行业的竞争程度和吸引力进行综合归纳。

波特确定的五种影响因素分别是：

- 供应商（向公司提供原料等物质的商户）的议价能力；
- 当前竞争对手的威胁；

- 新入市者（新进入市场的企业）的威胁；
- 买方的议价能力（大致相当于客户选择权）；
- 替代产品的威胁。

某一行业中，如果一家企业的商业模式比其竞争对手好，那么它的利润率就高于行业平均水平；如果它的商业模式不如其竞争对手，那么它的利润率就低于行业平均水平。

波特还研究了中区陷阱问题：在经验曲线模型中，为什么市场份额非常大或非常小的企业都能获得成功，而居中的企业却仅有偏低的利润率？

波特认为市场份额较大的企业遵循的是成本领先战略，即充分利用大批量生产*（大规模机械化生产）所带来的规模经济效应*（批量生产的产品越多，产品单价就越低），使自己产品的售价低于竞争对手的产品。而市场份额较小的企业则成功利用了市场细分*原理，它们成功找到了一个规模小但利润高的小众市场。

而居于中间地带的企业，既无法与市场份额较大的企业比拼成本，又无法同市场份额较小的企业比拼满足小众市场的能力，因此这些企业的盈利能力相对最弱。

时代贡献

波特在《竞争战略》中归纳的五力模型是当今用于理解如何在特定行业开展竞争的几种常用模型之一。

波士顿咨询集团的布鲁斯·亨德森曾于 1970 年提出一种叫做"增长率—占有率矩阵"*的方法，也称为"产品组合法"或"组合规划分析法"。这种方法把企业部门或产品依据市场份额和增长率排序。"现金牛"是指在低增速行业中占有较大市场份额的企业，这类企业通常投资少，不断被榨取利润。"瘦狗"是指在低增速行业中市场份额较小的企业，通常将被卖出。"明星"是指在高速增长的行业中占有较大市场份额的企业，需要注入较多资金以打败竞争对手。"问号"是指在高速增长的行业中占有较小市场份额的企业，这类企业会演变为上述三类企业之一。

这种方法的缺陷在于它主要关注市场份额和行业增长速度，对盈利能力关注不够，而提升盈利能力才是企业经营的目的所在。研究还表明，采用这种方法的企业的股东回报率低于不用这种方法的企业。[2] 许多商业教科书中已开始删除增长率—占有率矩阵模型。

另一种用于对竞争环境中的多种因素进行战略分析的理论框架叫做 PEST 分析法，即"政治、经济、社会和技术因素分析法"。政治因素包括税务政策等，经济因素包括利率等，社会因素包括某一经济体中消费者的老龄化速度等，技术因素包括技术变革的速度等。这一模型还有不同的变体，如考虑法律因素的 SLEPT 分析法、综合考虑环境和法律因素的 PESTLE 模型等。

---

1. 迈克尔·E.波特：《竞争战略：分析产业和竞争对手的技术》（第二版），纽约：自由出版社，1998 年，第 6 页。
2. 斯坦利·斯莱特和托马斯·兹维林："股东价值与一般投资搭配模型指导下的投资战略"，《管理学》第 18 卷，1992 年第 4 期，第 717—732 页。

第二部分：学术思想

5 思想主脉

要点 🔑

- 波特认为企业应该关注所处行业的五个关键因素：新入市者的威胁、替代产品的威胁、买方议价能力、供应商议价能力和业内竞争对手。

- 波特逐一细致分析了这些竞争因素，认为战略本质上就是如何取得并维持竞争优势的问题。

- 波特在《竞争战略》中使用的完全是针对商界人士的语言，基本不涉及专业术语、学术用语或数学知识。

核心主题

迈克尔·E. 波特的《竞争战略：分析产业和竞争对手的技术》的核心是研究新入市者、替代产品、买方议价能力、供应商议价能力和同行竞争强度对竞争的影响。

新入市者是指目前并不参与本行业竞争的公司。当他们看到这个市场有利可图时便可能进入，从而使竞争加剧，导致该行业中所有企业的盈利能力都下降。

替代产品是在消费者眼中类似或相近的产品。对于饮料生产商可口可乐公司而言，百事可乐是在软饮料市场与之争夺份额的竞争对手。但如果消费者转向饮用咖啡、能量型饮料、含酒精饮料或苏打水，那么软饮料市场就会整体扩大或缩小，因此上述都可被视为替代产品。

买方议价能力是指消费者的议价能力。如果买方有很多产品备选，或者市场中只有几个大买家，或者买家联手进行议价，那么买方的议价能力就较强。反之，如果大量小买家各自为政，那么他们的议价能力就较弱。买方议价能力强的典型例子就是 Groupon。这是一家网络公司，它代表自己的众多客户同其他公司协商，以获取低价。更极端的例子是买方垄断*，即市场上只有一个买家。英国国家医疗服务体系（NHS）就是这样的例子，它几乎是英国市场中唯一的医院设备采购商，所以能够获得优惠价格。美国的情况则不同，那里每家医院自行购买需要的设备。

供应商议价能力与买方议价能力密切相关，是指向其他公司销售原料和设备的企业的议价能力。供应商议价能力强的例子如下：如果公司的业务是烘烤面包，而市场上只有一家公司出售面粉，那么面包公司别无选择，只能向这家公司购买面粉；如果有多家面粉供应商，那么面包公司就可以货比三家，争取压低面粉售价。

最后，同行竞争是指某一领域内竞争对手彼此施压、争夺市场份额和利润的强度。在以下情况中，同行竞争比较激烈：竞争对手众多，彼此市场份额相似，消费者品牌忠诚度较低，产品差异化较小（即彼此替代性较强）。相反，如果行业快速增长，或者消费者的转换成本*较高（即消费者改用其他产品的代价较大，可能是由于消费者已经投资购买相关设备，而这些设备无法用于其他产品），这种情况下行业内的竞争可能就不太激烈。

> "竞争战略的目的在于帮助行业中的企业找到合理定位，从而能够最大限度地避免这些竞争因素所带来的不利局面，或使形势有利于自己。由于这些因素的综合作用会对所有企业都造成显而易见的影响，制定战略的关键在于深入分析每个因素的形成原因。"
>
> ——迈克尔·E. 波特：《竞争战略：分析产业和竞争对手的技术》

思想探究

波特逐一分析了这五种因素。他写道，"新入市者会扩大行业的产能，蚕食市场份额，并带来可观的新资源。"[1]从而导致行业中原有的企业售价降低，利润减少。另一方面，在行业中已占有相当市场份额的企业可以利用规模经济（一个产品量产的数量越多，该产品的单价就越低）的优势阻止新入市者加入竞争，迫使他们采用差异化战略。用波特的话说，就是"迫使新入市者投入大量资金来动摇现有客户的品牌忠诚度，这样做在初始阶段会要承受一定的损失，而且需要花费相当长的时间。"[2]

其次是替代产品带来的威胁。波特认为替代产品"对行业中企业可盈利的定价水平设定了上限，从而限定了该行业的潜在收益率。"[3]比如说，相对廉价且果糖含量高的玉米糖浆就可能给糖业企业设置了利润上限。其他因素，如转换成本（改用其他产品所需成本）等，可以减少此类威胁。

第三是买方的议价能力。同一行业中的各个公司不仅彼此竞争，而且还同买方竞争。波特写道，"买方极力压低产品售价，要求提高产品质量，提供更多服务，挑动卖方自相残杀，这些都将压缩整个行业的利润空间。"[4]波特认为公司的应对之策是有针对性地选择客户。"企业可以通过挑选最不具备议价能力的买方作为客户来提升自己在博弈中的地位。"[5]

第四是供应商的议价能力。供应商有可能提高原材料或服务的售价或降低其品质，从而对企业的竞争力构成威胁。如果企业无法将增加的成本转移给客户，其自身利润就会缩水。波特认为劳动力也是一种形式的供应商。"技能出色和／或依附于工会（维护工人

32

薪酬和劳动条件的组织）的员工可通过劳资谈判，大幅压缩企业的利润空间。"[6]

波特模型中最后一个因素是行业内的竞争对手。他写道，"某些竞争方式，尤其是价格竞争，往往难以预测，会使整个行业的盈利能力受损。"[7]同行竞争激烈程度的一个指标便是广告投入。大名鼎鼎的电脑和手机制造商苹果公司就设计广告攻击其主要对手——在软件和个人电脑领域独霸一方的微软公司。广告将苹果公司描绘成年轻时尚的代表，而微软公司则被描绘成中年书呆子的形象。另一个衡量指标是同行用于研发新技术的投入。

当市场中销量停滞或产品高度相似时，同行竞争最为激烈。波特认为公司应该设法改变这种局面。他指出，"将销售重点放在增长最快的产品上，有助于减轻来自同行的竞争压力。"[8]找到规避同行竞争的有效途径可以提高企业的利润率。

语言表述

波特明确表示，《竞争战略》是为从业人员（在一线从事企业管理或咨询的人士）所写。故而此书旨在为从事纯学术研究的学者和在商业一线打拼的商人建立沟通的渠道，亦即铺设商场实战和理论世界程式化模型之间的桥梁。

这一理念不但让该书语言浅显易懂，不含理论经济学中常用的数学和专业术语，也决定了其内容重点。在波特看来，用普通读者容易理解的语言撰写一本针对从业人员的作品使他有机会研究一些传统学术著作容易忽略的问题。他认为理论经济学主要关注行业状况，在抽象模型中每个企业都是相同的，这些模型也没有考虑到职业经理人的作用。

在《竞争战略》中，波特把研究范围拓展到了以下问题：行业的竞争实质对企业行为意味着什么？如何提高利润（这是企业关心的问题）而不是降低利润（这是社会、政府和消费者关心的问题）？如何理解相互影响的少数企业之间的竞争关系？

---

1. 迈克尔·E.波特：《竞争战略：分析产业和竞争对手的技术》（第二版），纽约：自由出版社，1998年，第7页。

2. 波特：《竞争战略》，第9页。

3. 波特：《竞争战略》，第23页。

4. 波特：《竞争战略》，第24页。

5. 波特：《竞争战略》，第26页。

6. 波特：《竞争战略》，第28页。

7. 波特：《竞争战略》，第17页。

8. 波特：《竞争战略》，第22页。

6 思想支脉

要点 🗝

- 波特在《竞争战略》中分析了五力模型 * 后，又阐释了三种策略，波特称之为通用战略 *。这些战略可以帮助企业在市场竞争中做出合理定位。

- 三种通用战略为：低成本战略、差异化战略和特定市场战略。

- 波特还分析了被广受忽略但极具潜力的小众市场，包括萎缩中的市场和正在加速进行全球化 * 扩张（业务扩张到其他大陆）的行业。

其他思想

迈克尔·E.波特的《竞争战略：分析产业和竞争对手的技术》一书的次要主题是研究企业如何通过以下三种策略之一在市场中获得竞争优势。这些策略分别是低成本、产品差异化和专注于特定群体。

低成本（波特称之为成本领先）的目标在于吸引价格敏感度最高的客户。他们品牌忠诚度较低，很容易被能够提供更低价格的竞争对手抢走。

差异化（一家公司的产品有别于其他公司出售的类似产品）主要针对价格敏感度不太高的客户，他们对现有市场的服务不够满意。差异化做得最好的通常是规模较大的公司。

规模较小的企业更适合采用特定市场战略，即锁定一个较小的受众市场，分析这些消费者的特殊需求。

这三项策略被波特称为"通用战略"，应该和他的五力模型综合使用，从而让企业找到市场竞争中最薄弱的环节。同样道理，企业也可以通过差异化策略——使自己的产品有别于竞争对手的产品——来重塑五大竞争因素；也可以通过投资来提高新入市者的准入门槛，具体做法包括对新技术申请专利保护（通过法律手段避免被侵权），或者大量投资购买设备。通过这一被称为定位 * 的做法，企业可以更好地适应周遭的竞争环境。

《竞争战略》首次提出，企业可以通过这一方法选择其战略。在此以前，由于受到知名战略家布鲁斯·亨德森作品的影响和对经验曲线的广泛认同，大家普遍认为存在一种适用于所有企业的战略——追求市场份额。

波特的重大创新之处在于指出企业真正应该追求的目标是盈利能力，而非市场份额，小企业同样可以获得高利润。这意味着企业可以选择不同的战略。

> "这些通用战略的有效实施需要企业完全投入以及配套的组织架构。如果企业有不止一个主要目标的话，支持力度就会被稀释。"
>
> —— 迈克尔·E. 波特：《竞争战略：分析产业和竞争对手的技术》

思想探究

在波特看来，价格领先（售价最低）策略"要求企业大量投资建设高效的生产设备，通过紧缩预算、压缩管理成本、避免客户欠账，尽量减少研发投入、售后服务、销售成本和广告支出的方式降低产品售价。"[1] 他写道，以低于竞争对手的价格出售产品"已成为这一战略的主旋律。"[2]

如果企业有较大市场份额的话，这种战略确实有效。波特认为，实施这一战略意味着初始阶段能够承受损失，因为要大量投资建厂，购买先进设备，以及以比较优惠的方式获得原料。

波特认为，这一战略对企业的强大吸引力在于它"可以使企业免受五种竞争因素的不利影响"。同买家和供应商讨价还价"只会稀释利润，直至在效率上稍逊一筹的竞争对手无利可图"。[3] 相对效率较低的企业在这一过程中会由于竞争压力而"首先遭罪"。[4]

企业可以通过提供最低价的产品或性价比最高的产品来吸引对价格敏感的客户。企业可以在资产管理上比竞争对手做得更好，比如航空公司可以提高飞机使用率，饭店可以提高清洁速度以便下一批顾客尽快入座。设备成本（即固定成本）如租金、人工费、照明费等均为沉没成本（已经付出）。如果能够提高产量，这些成本就可以由更多的产品分摊。

另一种战略则是提供朴实无华的标准化产品，就像爱尔兰的廉价航空公司瑞安航空＊一样。这种战略的缺点之一是客户忠诚度低，因为对价格敏感的客户一旦有更低价的选择，哪怕只是些许差别，就会转换门庭。

波特的第二个战略，即差异化战略，比较适合于大公司。这一战略主要针对那些对价格不太敏感，又对现有产品不太满意的客户。它营造出"整个行业内与众不同的感觉"。[5] 采用这种战略的企业应避免生产容易被竞争对手模仿的产品。要实施这一战略，企业必须拥有独特的技术、高素质的员工或者有关新技术的专利。

差异化战略可以有不同形式，如依靠优秀设计或顶级品牌（典型例子是德国豪车品牌梅赛德斯奔驰）。另一种方式是依靠出色的客户服务或可靠的分销网络。波特以美国建筑机械公司卡特培拉（Caterpillar Inc.）为例。[6] 该公司"不仅以分销网络发达和备件易得而著称，而且以其极为优质耐用的产品而闻名于世。"[7] 当然，"需要特别强调的是，差异化战略并不是说可以忽视成本因素，而只是说成本不是主要考虑的战略目标。"[8]

最后是特定市场战略，波特也称之为"专一化战略"，这对规模较小的企业尤为适用。较小的客户群体产生的销售量较少，不适合大公司专门为其调整在固定成本上的投资。特定群体可能和地理位置有关，也可能同人口特征（指特定人群，如特定年龄段或种族等）或生活习惯有关。[9]

这一战略主要关注特殊人群的特定需求。"专一化战略全在于对目标群体提供优质服务。"[10] 这样做的目的在于培养顾客对产品的忠诚度。这一战略的竞争优势源于创新和品牌营销，而非像低成本战略那样高度关注效率。

波特注意到这一针对特定市场的战略和其他两项战略也有关联。"尽管从总体而言这一战略并不侧重低成本或差异化，但在其特定市场内却体现出上述一种或两种战略的效果。"[11]

被忽视之处

《竞争战略》主要介绍了波特的五力模型，以及与之对应的三种通用战略。

当然，波特在书中也对某些特定行业的竞争态势提出了可资参考的见解。该书第 12 章对一些正在衰退的行业（如雪茄生产、书籍装订等）作了分析，第 13 章分析了一些正在快速全球化的行业（如现在的汽车制造业）。其他学者和从业者较少提及这些案例，而五力模型和三种通用战略则被世界各地的企业高管和咨询顾问反复提及，虽然他们有时理解未必完全正确。其实前述两类案例就颇具洞见。

举例而言，波特观察到传统观点认为处于夕阳行业＊（市场需求萎缩的行业）的业主应停止追加投资，尽量变现，最终歇业（售卖企业）。但波特也指出夕阳行业中企业的情况千差万别，其中一些通过大量追加投资后运营良好。要制定成功的战略，必须仔细分析剩余的需求情况。譬如说雪茄的总体需求在下降，但其高端市场（精制雪茄）的需求仍然存在，且这部分市场对价格并不敏感，容易接受新产品的高度差异化定位。有些夕阳行业的客户，如果转用其他产品的话得付出高昂的转换成本（购买新设备或用于培训的费用），例如改换计算机系统。

波特认为，随着全球化进程，为全球市场提供产品意味着更快的学习速度和更明显的规模效应（即产量越高，单个产品的成本越低）。如果许多国家都存在不满足于现有产品及服务的市场需求，企业就可以同时为这些分布于不同国家的特定市场提供服务。比如说，对任何一个国家来说，在"公平贸易"条件下（在严格的道德和环境标准下）生产的手机都属于小众市场，但放到全球范围就足以产生规模效应，让从事该项业务的企业有利可图。

---

1. 迈克尔·E. 波特：《竞争战略：分析产业和竞争对手的技术》（第二版），纽约：自由出版社，1998年，第35页。

2. 波特:《竞争战略》，第 35 页。

3. 波特:《竞争战略》，第 36 页。

4. 波特:《竞争战略》，第 36 页。

5. 波特:《竞争战略》，第 37 页。

6. 波特:《竞争战略》，第 37 页。

7. 波特:《竞争战略》，第 37 页。

8. 波特:《竞争战略》，第 37 页。

9. 波特:《竞争战略》，第 37 页。

10. 波特:《竞争战略》，第 38 页。

11. 波特:《竞争战略》，第 38—39 页。

7 历史成就

要点 🔑

- 波特的主要贡献在于他的理论已成为连接注重细节的商学院案例和高度抽象的经济学学术模型之间的桥梁。他称之为"中间地带理论框架"。

- 该书的另一特色在于它整合了行业组织经济学（主要关注企业和市场的结构）和商业政策（战略）两大领域的研究。虽然这两个领域都关注商业行为，但彼此以前并无关联。

- 该书仅做了中间层次的分析，并未涉及微观经济（企业内部）和宏观经济*（广义的经济体）的内容，这是该书的局限性。他在其后出版的《竞争优势：如何创造并保持骄人业绩》中补充了以上内容。

观点评价

为了更好地理解竞争要素，迈克尔·E.波特在《竞争战略：分析产业和竞争对手的技术》中提供了一种"中间地带理论框架"，它比单一企业或行业的案例分析更具普遍性，又比经济学模型更具体。

波特指出，"制定竞争战略的实质在于把企业和其周边环境综合考虑。"[1]《竞争战略》强调企业的战略选择。企业通过自我定位（对于其产品在市场中所处地位的战略考量）和赚取利润实现其战略。

值得指出的是，波特的五力模型和定位过程中的三个通用战略（低成本、差异化、特定市场）既不遵循商学院的案例分析方法，亦非经济学中的建模方式。波特称之为"框架"。他的解释是，"该框架力图用尽可能少的维度来分析极为复杂的现象。"[2]

波特的框架位于案例和模型之间，通过（波特自称）最少的"核心要素来反映竞争中的变量和维度"。[3] 框架的维度必须令人直觉上感到有理可依、有据可循，能够被从业人员（经商或商业咨询人士）认同。否则，这种框架只能用来显示专业咨询顾问的教育水准，说明咨询费物有所值。

> "通用战略这一章是最后完成的部分，因为这个领域多有争议。商学院的同事抱怨说'太抽象了'，'无法推广'，而经济学家则提出质疑，'数据分析呢？模型是什么？'跨出这一步很不容易。"
>
> —— 尼古拉斯·阿杰利斯和安妮塔·麦加恩：
> "迈克尔·E.波特访谈"，《管理者学会》

当时的成就

波特的《竞争战略》出版于 20 世纪 80 年代初，这是商业战略研究的重要转折期。在当时，这个新兴的领域提出了许多有趣的问题，却缺乏合适的理论框架来加以分析。[4]

20 世纪 60 年代到 70 年代初期，这方面的工作颇有起色。但70 年代末由于预期的成果未能如期而至，该领域的研究受到冷落。彼时日本企业（尤其是汽车制造业）空前成功。一位评论员写道："他们好像并不特别依靠规划，而是更多依靠产品质量、企业文化和民族精神以及生产管理。"[5]《竞争战略》的出版在商业战略领域掀起了第二波浪潮。

波特重点关注战略与竞争，旨在把这一学科引入新的方向。同时，他也吸收了前人的成果，其中包括前辈学者肯尼斯·安德鲁斯关于战略的价值以及企业高管在识别行业竞争威胁和机遇中的重要作用等学说。

波特吸收了从事战略研究的学者保尔·劳伦斯和杰伊·洛希的观点，他们认为对企业而言没有唯一正确的组织形式。波特在自己的战略与绩效分析（PIMS）中大量吸收了营销分析师西德尼·舍福勒的观点，并对调查数据所反映的中区陷阱作出了解释：高营业额和低营业额的企业都有机会获利，盈利能力不同于市场份额。波特认为企业应该追求的是利润。

该书出版以后，波特的思想在风云变幻的商界产生了经久不衰的影响力，被很多商界领袖所采纳。这充分反映了他受欢迎的程度。知名财经杂志《财富》把波特称为"有史以来最著名、影响力最大的商学院教授"。[6]

波特这本著作的特色之一是结合了行业组织和商业战略的研究，而两者结合正是吸引波特之处。波特先在哈佛商学院学习商业政策，然后以商业经济学专业博士生的身份师从经济学教授理查德·凯维斯*，研习行业组织。"这两个领域有许多交集，以前却没有真正的联系。"波特在接受采访时如是说。[7]

局限性

波特的理论框架虽然很成功，但仍有四点局限。其一，他的研究关注所谓的"中间层面"（介于宏观经济和微观经济之间），并未真正涉及宏观经济或微观经济。波特在其后续作品中拓展了研究领域，尤其是对价值链和集群（企业、供应商、劳动力的汇聚）的分析很大程度上弥补了这一缺陷。

其二，对公司性质考虑不多。波特的五力模型可以向公司提示某一市场的竞争因素是否有利、适宜公司竞争，但并未提及该公司是否适合在该市场中竞争。

其三，由于在经济学理论和商业实践之间寻找中间地带，波特提出的概念无法精准聚焦。譬如他曾提到，"企业如能向客户提供独特且有价值的产品，而不是一味寻求低价，就能使自己有别于竞争对手，取得差异化效果。"[8] 那究竟是企业还是产品实现了差异化呢？

最后一点，波特的模型为独家垄断*（某项产品或服务只有一个供应商）或寡头垄断*（只有少数几个供应商）提供了科学依据。在波特的模型中，出现以下情况完全正常：企业只根据自己的利益和对竞争因素的正确分析来决定如何定位。获得独家垄断地位或许对企业最为有利，但是否有利于其他社会群体就难说了，我们还指望通过市场竞争提高生产效率、降低产品售价呢。

1. 迈克尔·E.波特：《竞争战略：分析产业和竞争对手的技术》（第二版），纽约：自由出版社，1998年，第3页。

2. 尼古拉斯·阿杰利斯和安妮塔·麦加恩："迈克尔·E.波特访谈"，《管理者学会》第16卷，2002年5月第2期，第46页。

3. 阿杰利斯和麦加恩："访谈"，第46页。

4. 阿杰利斯和麦加恩："访谈"，第41—42页。

5. 罗伯特·E.安克利："迈克尔·波特的竞争优势和商业史研究"，《商业与经济史》第2卷，1992年第21期，第228—236页。

6. 杰夫·科尔文："坚定不移的迈克尔·波特"，《财富》，2012年10月15日，登录日期2016年2月9日，http://fortune.com/2012/10/15/theres-no-quit-in-michael-porter/。

7. 阿杰利斯和麦加恩："访谈"，第43—52页。

8. 波特：《竞争战略》，第120页。

8 著作地位

要点 ⚷━

波特毕生的学术研究都围绕着他在《竞争战略》(1980)中首次提出的观点而展开。他 1985 年出版的《竞争优势：如何创造并保持骄人业绩》从行业的角度对竞争进行了分析，1990 年出版的《国家竞争优势》一书从经济层面分析了国家之间的竞争。

在第二本书《竞争优势》中，波特引入了价值链的概念：企业用以增加价值和扩大竞争优势的行为和流程。

在第三本书中，波特介绍了集群的概念，即国家通过把某一行业的相关企业集中部署从而获得竞争优势，譬如好莱坞的影视业和伦敦金融城的金融业。

定位

　　1980 年出版的《竞争战略：分析产业和竞争对手的技术》是迈克尔·E. 波特出版的第一部著作，也是他读者最多、影响力最大的一部关于竞争的作品。以该书为基础，他开始了从不同角度研究竞争行为的极为成功的学术生涯。[1] 该书的基本内容源于他一年前在《哈佛商业评论》上发表的《竞争因素如何塑造战略》。[2] 这篇文章甫一发表就吸引了众多读者，并因被评为当年《哈佛商业评论》最佳文章而获得 1979 年麦肯锡奖第一名。文章的主要关注点在于企业如何分析行业环境并据此制定帮助企业走向成功的战略。

　　《竞争战略》之后，波特的大部分著作或多或少都建立在这本书的观点之上。波特的著作繁多，包括 19 本书和 125 篇文章，其中有两部重要著作广受好评，值得一提。

1985 年，波特在《竞争战略》后出版了《竞争优势：如何创造并保持骄人业绩》。[3]《竞争战略》从公司层面分析竞争，而《竞争优势》是从行业层面分析竞争。如果说第一本书的受众是年轻有为的管理层，那么第二本书的受众则是公司高层——企业老板。如果说《竞争战略》一书的任务之一是确定在竞争中保持领先地位的关键要素，那么《竞争优势》则力图指导企业如何保持领先地位。

《竞争优势》介绍了让波特声名鹊起的一个核心观点：价值链。价值链是一系列活动和过程的粗略模型，每个环节都在增值，顾客也要为此买单。企业的每个活动，下到培训和提供员工福利，都可以独立构成价值链的一个环节，形成和竞争对手相比的优势。

后来，波特在《国家竞争优势》（1990）一书中拓展了这一观点，探讨了国家之间如何在经济上进行竞争。他介绍的概念之一就是同一行业、同一地点的企业集群，比如像硅谷那样的科技中心。这让波特开始思考大规模的企业集群对国家竞争力的重要性。[4]

波特的其他著作将这三本主要著作的见解应用到不同的案例中，比如波特对于将竞争引入医疗卫生领域也做了很多探索。[5]他的很多其他著作都将其理论应用于特定的国家，比如日本和瑞典。[6]

> "最初我的研究领域是产业组织传统……后来我决定停止我所进行的研究并且跨越一大步……我决定寻找一个完整的框架，不仅利用统计检验，也利用我收集的大量案例。这就是《竞争战略》的起源。"
>
> ——尼古拉斯·阿杰利斯和安尼塔·麦加恩："迈克尔·E. 波特访谈"，《管理者学会》

整合

五力分析和三种通用战略（出自波特 1980 年出版的《竞争战略》）体现了波特对商界的主要贡献；价值链（出自 1985 年《竞争优势》）是波特另一广为人知的关键概念。

波特有的放矢地引入了价值链的概念："通过整体分析一个公司是无法理解其竞争优势的。竞争优势源于公司的很多分散活动：设计、生产、营销、交付和（售后）支持产品。每个活动都会影响公司的相对成本地位并形成差异化的基础。"[7]

这就是价值链，它不是一连串独立的活动（尽管每个活动可以被独立测量）。分析价值链有助于将公司拆分成一系列具有重要战略意义的过程，从而可以更好地理解每个活动对成本习性（产品成本根据公司生产活动的变动而改变的方式）和差异化的影响。相互独立的活动，如设计、生产、营销、交付等，如果能比竞争对手做得更好，就能为企业带来竞争优势。

波特的价值链概念很快就和《竞争战略》中的观点一起成为企业教科书和管理思想中的重要内容。此后，价值链的概念就被延伸至单个公司之外，人们通过接续分析企业供应商的供应商以及企业买方的买方，把价值链延展成一个"价值体系"*。

意义

波特在《竞争战略》中观点的重要意义主要体现在其第三本重要著作《国家竞争优势》（1990）一书中。在这本书中，波特对这些观点进行了深入的探索分析。

在《国家竞争优势》一书中，波特从国家层面分析竞争力以及影响竞争力的因素。美国企业竞争力的大幅、持久衰退让波特担忧不已，而大量证据的出现更印证了这种担忧。

在书中，波特进一步表达了对新古典经济学＊局限性的失望。新古典经济学是研究当今全球经济的主流方法，其基础假设是为实现特定目标的经济决策在本质上是理性的。他举的一个例子是产业集群：比如，科技行业在旧金山的硅谷迅速发展，而不是在工资水平和办公成本较低的地方；同样，金融业聚集在伦敦金融城，电影业聚集在好莱坞。在波特看来，集群的出现无法用主流经济理论解释；新古典主义经济学使用的过于简化的概念能产生非常好的模型，但其结论常常是无用的。

读者称赞波特1990年的著作是对过分简单化批评的明智回应，这些批评认为，如果其他国家比美国更具竞争力，那它们肯定得到了本国政府的帮助——在某种程度上，它们作弊了。[8] 相反，波特的著作鼓励美国思考如何在更现实、更诚信、更少意识形态和排外思维＊的基础上增强竞争力。

从那时起，他的核心论点——即各个国家参与国际竞争，而一个国家的竞争力是可以分析和衡量的——在管理学文献中占据了主导地位。然而，在经济学文献中则不然。在经济学家看来，国际竞争力是企业的特征，而不是国家的特征。对波特来说，这种对他眼中当今关键问题的忽视，恰恰让他坚定了对学院经济学的批评。

---

1. 参见伊恩·约根森："迈克尔·波特对战略管理的贡献"，《管理与会计》第5

卷，2008 年第 3 期，第 236—238 页。

2. 迈克尔·E. 波特："竞争因素如何塑造战略"，《哈佛商业评论》第 57 卷，1979 年第 2 期，第 137—145 页。

3. 迈克尔·E. 波特：《竞争优势：如何创造并保持骄人业绩》，纽约：自由出版社，1985 年。

4. 迈克尔·E. 波特：《国家竞争优势》，纽约：麦克米伦出版社，1990 年；第二版，1998 年。

5. 迈克尔·E. 波特和伊丽莎白·O. 泰斯伯格：《重新定义医疗：创造以结果为基础的价值竞争》，马萨诸塞州波士顿：哈佛商学院出版社，2006 年。

6. 迈克尔·E. 波特等：《日本还有竞争力吗？》，英国贝辛斯托克：麦克米伦出版社，2000 年；迈克尔·E. 波特等：《瑞典的竞争力》，斯德哥尔摩：诺斯泰特出版社，1991 年。

7. 波特：《竞争战略》，第 33 页。

8. 玛丽安·耶利内克："《国家竞争优势》书评"，《管理科学季刊》第 37 卷，1992 年第 3 期，第 507—510 页。

第三部分：学术影响

9 最初反响

要点 🔑

- 尽管波特的《竞争战略》引起了人们对管理和学术文献的极大兴趣,但也受到了一些批评。批评认为书中只选取了支持和阐释波特观点的例子,但实际上支持相反观点的例子也比比皆是。

- 虽然波特针对大部分批评都进行了详尽的回应,但他改变了在某一方面的立场:他现在相信"混合"战略——专注于低成本产品和小众市场的产品——也是有利可图的。

- 一些读者试图在波特五力分析模型的基础上增加第六种力量(通常是政府或科技);律师们声称,波特建议的旨在让新公司更难进入市场的许多举措可能违反了反垄断法 *(通过禁止企业联合统一定价等措施以促进自由市场竞争的法律)。

批评

针对迈克尔·E.波特《竞争战略:分析产业和竞争对手的技术》的主要批评有:

- 对于迅速变化的现代企业,其理解方法太僵化。
- 波特的通用战略是思想的替代品,而不能激发原创想法。
- 五力分析模型的根本理念是错误的。
- 波特的例子和引用的学术文献是有选择性且不完整的。
- 他的方法过于强调职业经理人和咨询顾问的作用,弱化了较低层次管理者和专家的直觉知识的作用,而这些人可能在制造和销售产品上经验更丰富,更了解实际情况。

第一种批评就是波特的模型太僵化了，并不适用于描述现代快速发展的产业。[1]"定位战"指的是生产者们争相占领低成本、高性能或小众市场，就像波特的通用战略中描述的那样。"定位战"适用于"耐用品"时代，那时有稳定的消费需求以及清晰的市场和竞争者。然而在现代商业世界，一批有代表性的批评者表示，"战略的精髓并不是公司产品和市场的结构，而是公司行为的动态变化。"从这个观点来看，万物都在变化，稳定的结构是不存在的。[2]

第二种批评是说，五力分析以及三种通用战略都是思想的替代品，而没有引发人们思考关键的问题。用一位批评者的话来说，"通用战略使得管理的任务突然变得更简单了。要想获得成功，你不必再苦苦摸索结构化的分析过程，你只需要依照机场书店的最新畅销书列出的清单就可以了。"[3]

第三种批评是，五力分析的根本理念可能是错误的。[4]五力分析的一个假设就是买方、竞争者和供应商三者是互不相关的，而且不会彼此协调，甚至没有互动。然而，在小型产业中，这三者会随时保持密切联系。在大型产业中，他们可能会在交易会上或通过产业协会进行互动。他们不仅仅是竞争关系，也会把对方看作支撑产业、促进产业健康发展和维护产业形象的同盟。如果他们私下关系紧密的话，公司可能会把潜在的竞争者看作援助或专业技能的来源，他们也可能会在产品需求量特别大时互相外包业务。

批评者们质疑的其他观点包括"企业界对未来有足够的掌握，并可以做出波特书中描述的战略规划"这一假设。同样，批评者们也质疑"公司的经济价值会因阻碍新公司进入市场的壁垒得到增长，而不是因资源或技能得到增长"这一假设；一些批评者认为这种观点"掩盖了员工在创新和创造价值方面的真正作用"。[5]

麻省理工学院的伯格·沃纳菲尔特*认为，如果不分析一家公司带给产业的资源，就不可能评估产业的吸引力，而这恰恰是五力分析的目标。沃纳菲尔特提出的资源基础理论*关注公司及其可用的资源，而不是产业本身。该理论把资源作为衡量竞争优势的出发点。[6]尽管波特的理论应用范围更广，但资源基础理论是其主要的竞争对手。

在阻碍新公司进入市场的壁垒问题上，商业学学者万斯·弗瑞德*和本杰明·欧维亚特*警告说，波特的理论"基本上忽视了美国的反垄断法"。反垄断法的目的是保护竞争，其手段包括禁止公司联合统一定价等。弗瑞德和欧维亚特称波特建议的部分措施违反了反垄断法。他们补充道，"波特探讨的大量防御性和补充性产品战略都有可能违反反垄断法，而波特对此视而不见。"[7]他们表示，波特推荐的让潜在竞争者难以进入市场的很多措施，都可能违反谢尔曼法*（1890年通过的美国反垄断立法中的重要法案）。[8]

第四种批评认为，波特选择性地使用例子和引用学术文献。商业研究教授威廉·加特纳*表示，波特没有公平地选取例子，而是专门选择了支持和诠释其观点的例子。加特纳说，"有一种可能性就是其他例子可能会推翻波特的观点，而这也许会带来一些非常好的研究。"[9]

该批评还认为，波特对战略管理文献（尤其是哈佛商学院以外的研究机构的文献）或多或少持有选择性观点。加特纳说，"波特给出的情景构建战略说服力并不强，他只需看一下查尔斯河对面，就会知道麻省理工学院研究情景构建（系统动态）已有20年了。"[10]情景构建是一种分析未来发展趋势（即情景）的战略制定方法，该方法让规划者思考三种不同的趋势：乐观的、悲观的和可能的。

最后，加拿大学者亨利·明茨伯格 * 提出了另一种强调应急战略 * 的方法。应急战略是指临时出现的作为高级管理层正式战略的替代或补充的战略。这是针对"波特的方法太过依赖于高级管理层决策"这一批评的回应。一位批评家说，"鉴于这些战略专家的高度专业性和高级别岗位，"波特的框架会阻碍"任何促进参与式管理的举措。"[11]（参与式管理是指企业结构内各个层级的人都可以在公司管理中发挥作用。）

> "波特的著作充斥着渴望被拿去应用的想法。"
> —— 威廉·加特纳：《竞争战略》与《竞争优势》书评，
> 《管理学会评论》

回应

在第二版《竞争战略》中，波特对上述批评进行了回应。

第一种批评是针对波特的五力分析最常见的批评，即五力分析模型无法分析和解释产业变化。波特对此回应说，"模型并不是静止的，这个框架的每一部分——产业分析、竞争者分析、竞争性定位——都强调了不断变化的情况。"[12]

一些支持波特的研究者试图把时间加入模型当中来进一步改进他的模型。[13] 其中一例就是评估五种竞争因素在过去、现在以及未来一定时间内的一致性，以及检验产业结构是保持相对稳定还是快速变化。

波特认同明茨伯格应急战略一说，应急战略确实可能存在。对他来说，"在某一产业竞争的每家公司都有竞争战略，不论是隐性的还是显性的。竞争战略可能是通过规划显性制定的，也可能是通过公司不同的职能部门活动隐性发展而来的。"[14] 然而，波特称，任何一家追求"通过专业导向和激励措施来决定所采取的方法"的公司中，应急（或隐性）战略可以来源于公司的每一个职能部门。对波特而言，这种应急战略不如公司高层制定的总体政策管用。"这些部门方法的总和通常并非最佳战略。"[15]

批评者强调波特选择性地运用学术文献和例子，并且指出，诸如政府政策这样的第六种力量也会影响市场以及公司的竞争地位。波特否定了这一看法，并表示"政府的力量和影响与产业的盈利能力之间是没有（恒定）关系的。你不能说，'政府的影响力大，产业的盈利能力就低'，或者'政府的影响力小，产业的盈利能力就高。'"[16]

有些批评认为波特的五力分析是不完整的，对此，支持《竞争战略》的读者建议应该增加第六种力量，这种力量可以是政府或科技，已经有读者用这种方式去拓展波特的研究。一个典型的例子就是商业学学者亚当·布兰登勃格*和拜瑞·内勒巴夫*利用博弈论*（关于冲突与合作的数学模型，用于研究理性决策者的互动）拓展了《竞争战略》的观点。

布兰登勃格和内勒巴夫分析了供应相关产品的企业之间的关系，并用分析结果来解释企业间战略同盟背后的动态，[17] 他们把这些互补性产品（而不是竞争性产品）称为"互补者"*。典型例子是：热狗和小圆面包；杜松子酒和奎宁水。

尽管波特否定了大多数相关尝试，但是他却对布兰登勃格和内勒巴夫将其研究拓展到战略同盟的工作表示赞赏。波特仍然坚信，政府或科技的作用必须通过其与五力的协同作用来理解。[18]

然而，波特修订了他对混合企业战略是否存在的想法。混合企业战略是指一家公司同时采用低成本战略和差异化战略（满足特定市场的需求）。[19] 一些早期的证据表明，同时采用两种战略的公司要比只采用一种战略的公司更加成功。[20]

冲突与共识

学者们基本认可波特的著作对过去 20 年产业公司研究的实用经验做了精辟总结。经济学家们大多把《竞争战略》作为一种有用的理论和假说来源，而且此后的学术项目可以进一步验证波特的观点。商业和管理学学者把《竞争战略》看作研究的起点。还有一些作者建议拓展或调整书中的一些内容。2013 年发表于《哈佛商业评论》的一篇文章中写道，"迈克尔·E. 波特的五力分析永久性地改变了这一领域。"[21]

对波特观点的进一步研究工作，其文献主要发表在如《战略管理期刊》这样的杂志上。该杂志之所以成立，很大一部分原因是由于波特的《竞争战略》问世后，人们对这一话题产生了极大兴趣。

作为一本受到广泛使用的商学院教科书，《竞争战略》当然免不了被频繁抨击。自 2008 年以来，很多人都质疑，在受政府管制、从而规避竞争的市场以外，是否真正存在长期竞争优势。[22]那些对 2008 年金融危机 * 爆发前的公司经营提出强烈批评的人就进一步强调长期战略优势不可能存在，这只是专业管理咨询阶层的一种假想。

人们仍在探索替代方法，这其中就包括资源基础理论。波特的五力分析仍然被人们广泛传阅和使用，但在众多理论当中，资源基础理论是最有力的竞争者。

1. 格雷戈里·德斯等:《战略管理》,伦敦:麦格劳-希尔出版社,1995年。

2. 乔治·斯托克等:"能力竞争:公司战略的新规则",《哈佛商业评论》第70卷,1992年第2期,第57—69页。

3. 克利夫·鲍曼:"通用战略:思想的替代品?",《阿什里奇学刊》,2008年春,第1页。

4. 凯文·科恩和索姆·苏拉马尼亚姆:"为战略制定规章制度",《麦肯锡季刊》,1996年第4期,第14—25页。

5. 奥马尔·阿克托夫:"迈克尔·波特战略管理框架的错误期望",《管理学问题与观点》,2005年第4期,第181—200页。

6. 伯格·沃纳菲尔特:"以资源为基础的企业分析",《战略管理期刊》第5卷,1984年第2期,第171—180页。

7. 万斯·弗瑞德和本杰明·欧维亚特:"迈克尔·波特漏掉的一章:触犯反垄断法的风险",《管理者学会》第3卷,1989年第1期,第49—56页。

8. 弗瑞德和欧维尔特:"迈克尔·波特漏掉的一章",第49页。

9. 威廉·加特纳:《竞争战略》和《竞争优势》书评",《管理学会评论》第10卷,1985年第4期,第874页。

10. 加特纳:"书评",第875页。

11. 阿克托夫:"错误期望",第198页。

12. 迈克尔·E.波特:《竞争战略:分析产业和竞争对手的技术》(第二版),纽约:自由出版社,1998年,第xv页。

13. 泽米尔·杜乐奇等:"从五个竞争力到五个合作力:关于产业结构与公司间相互联系的进一步观点",《Procedia——社会和行为科学》第58卷,2012年,第1077—1084页。

14. 波特:《竞争战略》,第xxi页。

15. 波特:《竞争战略》,第xxi页。

16. 尼古拉斯·阿杰利斯和安妮塔·麦加恩:"迈克尔·E.波特访谈",《管理者学会》第16卷,2002年第2期,第46页。

17. 亚当·布兰登勃格和拜瑞·内勒巴夫:《合作竞争》,纽约:皇冠出版集团,1996年。

18. 波特:《竞争战略》,第xv页。

19. 丹尼尔·I.普拉约戈:"竞争战略与产品质量之间的关系",《产业管理与数据系统》第 107 卷，2007 年第 1 期，第 69—83 页。

20. 彼得·赖特等："战略概况、市场份额和业绩"，《产业管理》，1990 年，第 23—28 页。

21. 迈克尔·赖亚尔："竞争的新活力"，《哈佛商业评论》，2013 年，第 80—87 页。

22. 史蒂夫·丹宁："迈克尔·波特的摩立特集团为何倒下？真正重要的力量"，《财富》，2012 年 11 月 20 日，登录日期 2016 年 1 月 24 日，http://www.forbes.com/sites/stevedenning/2012/11/20/what-killed-michael-porters-monitor-group-the-one-force-that-really-matters/#d4b96f2733c7。

10 后续争议

要点 ⚷——

- 波特的观点推动了一系列工具的发展和广泛应用，这些工具是用来测量五力分析模型中的五种竞争因素的。比如四企业集中度 * 可用于衡量市场份额，赫芬达尔—赫希曼指数 * 可用于衡量企业在市场中的地位。

- 2008 年金融危机后，波特的观点遭到了大量抨击，尤其是"竞争优势在没有政府管制的情况下也能长期保持"的观点。

- 尽管波特反驳了这些批评，但他的确表示，如果今天他来写这本书，他会把关注点放在对买方议价能力的新研究上。

应用与问题

迈克尔·E.波特在《竞争战略：分析产业和竞争对手的技术》中提出的五力分析和三种通用战略——成本领先战略（保持产品低价）、差异化战略和专一化战略——在战略管理界得到了高度认可。学者们对这些观点都进行了大量的实验和理论分析。[1]

这些理论简洁有力，因而长盛不衰。汽车制造商在 20 世纪 80 年代应用了波特的方法，今天硅谷的初创企业（加利福尼亚州的新科技公司）也在应用这些理论。波特的模型促使商业领袖们去思考竞争和盈利能力，而不被旧方法中过时的关注点分散注意力。正如《经济学人》的一位作者所说："很少有管理学的观点如此清晰且符合直觉。"[2] 波特的方法是如此清晰明了，可以轻松应用于各种情境；它抓住了竞争的要义。

波特的理论框架促使企业界提出问题，这使得一些衡量企业特征的工具得到了广泛应用。其中一例就是采用三种指标来衡量竞争对手，竞争对手是五力分析中的一种因素。另一例是四企业集中度，衡量四家最大的企业的市场份额。其他的例子还有赫芬达尔—赫希曼指数和勒纳指数*，这两者都可用于评估一家公司在市场中的地位。上述指数虽然在《竞争战略》出版前就已存在，却因为这本书更加流行。

如今互联网飞速发展，科技日新月异，波特的模型在多大程度上适用于今天复杂的商业环境？这引起了广泛的讨论。同时，近期基于数据的研究发现五力分析和企业业绩紧密相关。比如，2014年的一份统计研究显示，波特的五力分析模型可以很好地解释肯尼亚合作银行的业绩。[3]

> "除非政府实行管制，否则持续竞争优势是根本不存在的。"
> —— 史蒂夫·丹宁："迈克尔·E. 波特的摩立特集团为何倒下？真正重要的力量"，《福布斯》

思想流派

然而，2008年金融危机爆发后，波特关于持续竞争优势的观点遭到猛烈抨击。[4] 在这一点上，波特和其他很多管理学专家无异，都受到了来自公众和媒体的大量批评，指责他们对经济下行负有不可推卸的责任。

2008年金融危机引发了占领运动*，示威者抗议经济不平等和银行活动对社会造成的伤害。在这样的政治环境中，像波特这样的知名人士自然成为众矢之的。

2012 年摩立特集团的破产和 1.16 亿美元的贱卖更加剧了此类批评的声音。摩立特集团是波特和五名哈佛同事于 1983 年创办的一家商业战略咨询公司。众多批评者中，风险投资家 * 彼得·戈尔斯基 * 写道，"一只蒙着眼睛扔飞镖的大猩猩也可以像波特这样的高薪顾问一样，在五力分析框架中选出同样水平的商业战略。"[5]（"风险投资家"是指为创业公司提供初期投资，期待在企业成功后获利的投资人。）

一种批评认为，《竞争战略》在其目标和行动策略上都是有缺陷的。《竞争战略》的目标是寻找长期超额利润的机遇：通过壁垒防止竞争者的出现，从而使自己处于低竞争的舒适环境中。波特提出的这些机遇对追求盈利的公司来说是一条捷径，但许多经济学家对可能产生的高盈利表示担忧，认为这可能会让消费者承担不公平的成本。前管理学顾问马修·斯图尔特 * 和其他批评者表示，不是用心去设计更好的产品和服务，长期为消费者和社会带来更多价值，而是寻求低竞争环境，这是一条投机取巧的成功之路。[6]

这些批评者还认为，波特的方法是有缺陷的。他们表示，除非在政府管制的情况下（比如政府授予某一电信服务供应商或航空公司垄断地位），否则长期竞争优势是不存在的。同时，持续高于平均水平的利润也是不可能从企业结构中预测出来的。斯图尔特在《管理学神话：解读现代企业哲学》（2009）一书中写道，波特的理论能够解释过去取得的成功，但是"基本不可能用于预测未来的成功"。[7]然而，不是所有人都接受这种批评。《华尔街日报》就称这种批评"聪明但不公平"。《华尔街日报》表示，波特为帮助人们理解企业竞争环境作出的贡献要比斯图尔特认为的大得多。[8]

事实上，在《竞争战略》这本书出版 30 年后，波特还饱受争议，这本身就说明了这本书在商业界和管理学界举足轻重的地位。

当代研究

《竞争战略》最近得到应用的一些例子包括 2015 年开展的学术研究，研究主题是幼儿园[9]和日本啤酒市场的竞争战略。[10]

波特表示，如果现在他重写《竞争战略》这本书，他会调整五力分析模型，从最近对买方议价能力的研究着手。[11]他说要把需求侧规模经济（比如网络效应*或从众效应*）纳入其中。某商品或服务的一位用户会对该商品或服务相对于其他用户的价值产生影响（因该商品或服务的价值取决于用户数量），这就是网络效应。电话就是一例（一位电话用户会给不同的人打电话），社交网络也是如此（用户会与其他人互动和分享图片）。从众效应和网络效应类似——产品越普及，用户就会越多。比如，当人们看到朋友在使用一种新科技，比如 2007 年首次亮相的 iPhone，他们就会考虑要不要也入手一个 iPhone。人们对商品的需求会随着这种商品普及程度的提高而增加。

---

1. 彼得·赖特："细化波特的战略"，《战略管理期刊》第 8 卷，1987 年第 1 期，第 93—101 页。

2.《经济学人》报刊编辑："竞争优势"，2008 年 8 月 4 日，登录日期 2016 年 2 月 9 日，http://www.economist.com/node/11869910。

3. 克里斯托弗·印迪斯："波特的五力模型在组织业绩中的应用：以肯尼亚合作银行为例"，《欧洲商业与管理期刊》第6卷，2014年第16期，第75—85页。

4. 史蒂夫·丹宁："迈克尔·E.波特的摩立特集团为何倒下？真正重要的力量"，《财富》，2012年11月20日，登录日期2016年1月24日，http://www.forbes.com/sites/stevedenning/2012/11/20/what-killed-michael-porters-monitor-group-the-one-force-that-really-matters/#d4b96f2733c7。

5. 丹宁："迈克尔·E.波特的摩立特集团为何倒下？"。

6. 马修·斯图尔特：《管理学神话：解读现代企业哲学》，纽约：W. W.诺顿出版社，2009年，第191页。

7. 斯图尔特：《管理学神话》，第194页。

8. 菲利普·德尔夫斯·布劳顿："冒牌理论，对生意有害无益"，《华尔街日报》，2009年8月5日，登录日期2016年1月24日，http://www.wsj.com/articles/SB10001424052970204313604574329183846704634。

9. 陈怡靖："不同特征幼儿园的竞争策略与家长满意度之间的关系"，《全球商业管理》第11卷，2015年第2期，第76—87页。

10. 山本菅："麒麟：日本啤酒市场的商业策略"，麻省理工学院斯隆管理学院工商管理硕士论文，2015年。

11. 尼古拉斯·阿杰利斯和安妮塔·麦加恩："简介：迈克尔·E.波特的'竞争战略'"，《管理者学会》第16卷，2002年第2期，第41—42页。

11 当代印迹

要点 ⚷━

- 如今在商业战略和竞争领域，波特的《竞争战略》仍是最重要、被引用最多的著作之一。

- 曾有学者得出了和波特相似的结论，但不及他有名；《竞争战略》也许是因其声名显赫而遭到诸多批评。

- 在学术上，波特提供的不是一种以个人经验为依据的单一观点，而是一个框架，以及供研究者验证此框架的丰富理论，因而《竞争战略》也催生了一大批后续研究成果。

地位

《竞争战略：分析产业和竞争对手的技术》一书在商业领域（尤其是商业战略领域）产生了重大影响。迄今为止，迈克尔·E. 波特已写了 19 部著作和 125 篇学术论文[1]，他曾在哈佛商学院为几代一流管理者与咨询师授课，他的竞争战略理念是全世界商科课程的重要组成部分。[2] 在哈佛期间，他曾任战略与竞争研究院院长，如今该研究院致力于将波特的研究成果应用于实际的商业运作中。

不过，波特最有名的还是《竞争战略》这本书。他在职业生涯后期不断完善和发展自己的理念，这些理念的核心就包含在这本书中。《竞争战略》先后印刷 63 次，以 19 种语言出版。波特所著的《竞争优势：如何创造并保持骄人业绩》（1985）已至少印刷 38 次。

《竞争战略》也为探索企业在实际环境中如何应对竞争压力提供

了丰富的观点和理论，在实际环境中，企业的竞争更加艰难。波特对商业产生的影响并不局限于他个人的著作，其他受波特观点启发的学者所著的作品同样影响深远。谷歌学术有一项专门的工具记录学术作品的引用次数，其中，《竞争战略》一书的引用次数高达 6.5 万。[3]

> "我永远不会忘记，一位资深教授对我说，他认为我对五力分析模型所做的笔记是'一项失败了的出色实验'。"
>
> —— 尼古拉斯·阿杰利斯和安妮塔·麦加恩：
> "迈克尔·E. 波特访谈"，《管理者学会》

互动

如今在商业战略领域，波特的五力模型无疑是最著名且应用最广的模型之一，或许正因如此，对它的批评之声也从未断绝。

最常见的批评是说，波特选择这五大要素并没有特别站得住脚的理由。[4]还有人对其能否很好地适应现代商业环境表示质疑，毕竟现代商业环境愈发复杂、瞬息万变、扑朔迷离。波特五力模型似乎不能有效预测准入门槛、供应链关系、新入市者等因素如何变化，这些变化往往十分迅速，毫无预警。

还有一些比较有趣的评论，稍稍偏向理论层面。加拿大的商业战略研究者亨利·明茨伯格指出，从理论上看，低成本与其他类型的差异化并没有什么不同，只是差异化的一种形式。差异化的类型和范围，才应当是制定战略需要关注的两个维度。[5]

持续争议

值得一提的是，大量基于实际数据展开的工作都始于波特的

《竞争战略》。

韩国学者金麟洙*和林允哲*1998 年基于对韩国公司的研究撰写的《快速发展国家的环境、通用战略和绩效：一种分类学方法》一文有力地证实了波特的理论。这两位韩国学者发现，相比其他理论，《竞争战略》中的通用战略与他们的数据最为契合。[6]

得出同样结论的还有商业研究者亚历山大·米勒*和格里高利·戴斯*，他们 1993 年在《管理学研究》发表文章《对波特模型（1980）的概括性、准确性和简单性进行评估》。[7]战略与绩效分析（PIMS）是经过 20 年研究得出的分析影响市场因素的模型，两位学者将波特通用战略和战略与绩效分析的结果进行对比，发现尽管波特的模型比较简单，却能抓住复杂问题的关键。

同样作为宽泛型框架，资源基础理论是波特战略观的主要竞争对手，它把企业视为"各类独特资源的集合体"。[8]两种理论各有所长。波特五力模型侧重外部分析，研究市场环境；资源基础理论侧重内部分析，研究公司业务、人力、科技和自然资源等的特殊性。也有人试过创造一个新模型，把这两种方法结合起来。[9]

近年来，许多学者尝试进一步发展波特的理论框架。最著名的便是"金三角模型"*，该模型由麻省理工学院管理和战略研究者阿诺尔多·哈克斯*与迪恩·怀尔德*提出，主要研究公司和顾客之间的纽带对持续盈利的影响。与之前把竞争（甚至是产品本身）看作关键因素的理念不同，"金三角模型"关注的是在透明与公平的原则下与公司保持长期联系的顾客。受此理念影响的研究也更多关注制定促进"锁定顾客"的发展战略，即将顾客与公司"绑定"，并消除顾客被竞争对手"绑定"的机会[10]。一个典型的例子就是积分卡，另一个方法就是采用先进的计算机工具持续追踪常客。

1. 迈克尔·波特："简历"，登录日期 2016 年 2 月 8 日，www.kozminski.edu.pl/ uploads/import/kozminski/pl/default_opisy_2/3269/1/1/m._porter_-_kandydat_do_tytulu_ doktora_honoris__causa_alk.doc。

2. 杰夫·科尔文："坚定不移的迈克尔·波特"，《财富》，2012 年 10 月 15 日，登录日期 2016 年 1 月 23 日，http://fortune.com/2012/10/15/theres-no-quit-in-michael-porter/。

3. 谷歌学术："波特战略管理"，登录日期 2016 年 1 月 23 日，https:/scholar.google. com/scholar?q=Porter+Competitive+Strategy&btnG=&hl=en&as_sdt=0%2C9。

4. 约翰·奥肖内西：《战略营销：战略手段》，马萨诸塞州波士顿：爱伦与昂温出版社，1984 年；理查德·J. 斯皮德："噢，波特先生！重新评估竞争战略"，《营销情报与策划》第 7 卷，1989 年第 5/6 期，第 8—11 页。

5. 亨利·明茨伯格："通用战略：构建全面框架"，罗伯特·兰姆和保罗·什里瓦斯塔娃编：《战略管理进展》第 5 卷，康涅狄格州格林威治：JAI 出版社，1988 年，第 1—67 页。

6. 金麟洙和林允哲："快速发展国家的环境、通用战略和绩效：一种分类学方法"，《管理学会学报》第 31 卷，1998 年第 4 期，第 802—827 页。

7. 亚历山大·米勒和格里高利·戴斯："对波特模型（1980）的概括性、准确性和简单性进行评估"，《管理学研究》第 30 卷，1993 年，第 553—585 页。

8. 苏珊妮·里瓦德等："资源基础观与竞争战略：信息技术对企业绩效贡献的综合模型"，《战略信息系统》第 15 卷，2006 年第 1 期，第 29—50 页。

9. 扬尼斯·斯帕诺斯和斯派罗斯·洛卡斯："租房一代的因果逻辑考察：波特的战略框架与资源基础观的对比"，《战略管理》第 22 卷，2001 年第 10 期，第 907—993 页。

10. 阿诺尔多·哈克斯：《金三角模型：重构你的商业战略》，纽约：斯普林格出版社，2009 年。

12 未来展望

要点 🗝

- 互联网、全球化（各国不断增强的经济、社会、政治联系）与解除管制＊（政府对市场运作减少干预）都刺激了竞争。那么，波特的理论究竟是过时了还是更有指导意义了？批评者和支持者为此争论不休。

- 自 1980 年《竞争战略》问世起，波特就一直拥有巨大的影响力，原因之一是他的五力模型很好地对应了微观经济学（个人和社区层面的经济行为）的核心内容，这些内容不会轻易过时。

- 波特的理念影响深远，广为传播。在如今的管理行为中，尤为重要的是正确理解这些理念——包括其局限和受到的质疑——并分辨这些理念在哪些情况下不适用。

潜力

如今，商业环境瞬息万变，迈克尔・E.波特的《竞争战略：分析产业和竞争对手的技术》一书对理解和预测商业竞争颇有助益。互联网、全球化、解除管制（诸如哪些企业可以参与市场竞争等问题，政府将不再管制）等当前趋势将如何影响未来？他的五力模型为此提供了清晰的思路。

与过去相比，如今企业可以获得更多关于顾客、供应商和竞争对手的信息，尤其是通过互联网。

一方面，企业可以更加容易地搜集信息增强竞争力，比如运用五力分析。另一方面，企业处理起竞争问题来也会更加复杂，因为竞争因素变得愈发激烈了：比如，顾客能够更加容易地找到替代品，顾客更换企业的成本会降低，价格也更为透明。

但与此同时，互联网能够极大地推动商业发展，促使企业不断完善订单自动处理与顾客关系管理系统，在竞争中更好地体现差异化。如果企业采取"小众市场战略"，互联网能助其更加精准地了解目标市场的需求。

此外，全球化和解除管制这两个重要趋势也值得深思。全球化拓展了全球市场，加剧了基于价格的竞争，颠覆了依照地理位置布局当地市场的旧策略（独立的街头小店模式的消亡就证实了这一点）。而解除管制——撤销政府管制以推动竞争——使得新公司更容易进入以前竞争受限的市场。

批评者指出，互联网、全球化和解除管制已然使波特模型失效，或者至少需要大幅修正。在《竞争战略》第二版的引言中，波特回应道，即使不做更新，他的五力模型仍可解释上述三大趋势。[1]

> "医疗行业改革，关键在于将竞争与对病人而言的价值联系起来。医疗行业的价值就是，每一块钱的医疗成本所能够达到的医疗效果。如果医疗体制下的所有参与者都以价值为基础进行竞争，那么整体的医疗价值就会迅速改善。"
>
> —— 迈克尔·E.波特：《重新定义医疗：创造以结果为基础的价值竞争》

未来方向

《竞争战略》中的五力模型长期适用，一个理由就是它们分别对应着微观经济学的重要内容。

"供应商的议价能力"对应供求理论*、成本与生产理论*和价

70

格弹性*，而这都和价格与市场作用力间的关系密切相关。"买方 /
顾客的议价能力"同样对应价格和市场这两个作用力，价格和市场
受消费者行为*影响，同时影响着消费者行为。

"当前市场参与者的竞争"对应市场结构*、市场上参与者或经
济主体的数量、市场规模和增长率*（一段时间内某经济体中商品
和服务的市场价值的增长），"替代品的威胁"对应替代效应*（当
一种商品价格上升时，顾客倾向于购买其他价格更低的替代品），
"新入市者的威胁"对应市场准入壁垒*——即阻碍企业进入一个新
市场的因素，如管制或专利。

批评者如《超越波特》的作者拉里·唐斯*认为，和 20 世纪
80 年代初相比，现在的诸多因素如信息技术（计算机和互联网）、
全球化、解除管制等，都需要不同的商业工具去分析。[2] 但波特的
支持者认为，之前的错误正是由于过分夸大了如今的数字经济和以
前的传统经济的区别，比如互联网公司夸大了收益预期，投资者大
幅抬高股价，导致出现了互联网泡沫*，最后股价大幅跳水，甚至
有的公司在 20 世纪 90 年代后期轰然倒闭。

波特支持者的另一个反驳理由是，拉里·唐斯的观点自相矛盾。
他认为波特的模型太过依赖 20 世纪 80 年代的经济状况，但他指出的
最重要因素如今可能很快就会被新的因素所取代，比如可穿戴技术和
3D 打印等新科技，或为环保目的而出台的新形式的管制。评估波特五
力模型最重要的一点，是看它是否只基于当时的经济状况，还是符合
长远的经济发展实际，并且在下一次数字技术繁荣到来之时依然适用。

小结

在所有的商业和管理类书籍中，《竞争战略》取得今日的地位当

之无愧。《金融时报》评出的全球排名前 20 的工商管理硕士项目均把波特五力模型纳入其战略管理课程。[3] 另一个相关理论方法是资源基础理论，出自伯格·沃纳菲尔特的文章《以资源为基础的企业分析》，[4] 但其影响力不可与五力模型同日而语。在谷歌搜索记录中，五力模型的点击量要比它的头号竞争对手资源基础理论多 260 万次。

《竞争战略》指出，企业要想获利，要么降低成本，要么差异化，舍此别无他途。

波特的五力模型为企业评估商业环境提供了一个简单实用的框架。同样，他的三大通用战略清晰地列出了企业同对手竞争的可选方案。

尽管批评者们也提出了一些观点，比如不要简单使用千篇一律的方法制定战略，但是自《竞争战略》问世的 25 年来，波特的理念仍被奉为商业战略管理界的"圣经"。

理解和运用迈克尔·E. 波特卓越的工具和理念固然重要，但理解其局限性和其受到的批评性声音，并且分辨什么情况下这些工具和理论不适用同样重要——这对于商业战略的初学者来说尤为关键。

---

1. 迈克尔·E. 波特：《竞争战略：分析产业和竞争对手的技术》（第二版），纽约：自由出版社，1998 年，第 xv 页。

2. 拉里·唐斯："超越波特"，《情境》，1997 年 12 月。

3. 阿米尔·塞尚："限制五大力量"，《商业智能战略》，2013 年 11 月 19 日，登录日期 2016 年 1 月 24 日，http://www.bi.edu/bizreview/articles/conning-the-five-forces-/。

4. 伯格·沃纳菲尔特："以资源为基础的企业分析"，《战略管理期刊》第 5 卷，1984 年第 2 期，第 171—180 页。

术语表

1. **反垄断法**：旨在促进自由市场竞争的法律，它制止反竞争行为，如多个公司之间达成协议统一定价。著名的反垄断法有 1890 年美国谢尔曼法案、1914 年克莱顿法案和 1951 年欧洲煤钢共同体协议。

2. **从众效应（也称乐队花车效应）**：一种购买产品的人数越多，产品就越受欢迎的模式；个人购买产品的概率随着其他已购买消费者数量增多而上升。

3. **波士顿咨询公司**：1963 年成立于波士顿的著名管理咨询公司。1968 年，该公司创建了增长率—占有率矩阵。公司创始人布鲁斯·亨德森是经验曲线及其对战略的影响的积极倡导者。

4. **产业集群映射项目**：波特在哈佛商学院领导的一个项目，开始于 2014 年，目标是收集美国区域经济中的集群数据。集群是指相关企业的区域集中，集群映射旨在帮助地区和企业更好地了解他们的竞争地位。

5. **集群**：企业、供应商和劳动力在某地的集聚。迈克尔·E.波特在 1990 年出版的《国家的竞争优势》一书中推广了这一术语。这样的例子包括技术行业的硅谷、金融行业的伦敦金融城和葡萄酒行业的法国勃艮第或波尔多地区。

6. **比较优势**：英国经济学家大卫·李嘉图于 1817 年首次提出的理论。根据这一理论，国家和其他经济行为者会专门生产最有利可图的商品（能以最低边际成本生产的商品），同时参与国际贸易购买其他的商品。

7. **竞争**：卖家之间为提高利润、市场份额和销售量而进行的较量。古典经济学家（比如英国经济学家亚当·斯密在其 1776 年的《国富论》中）认为竞争可以激励企业创新，提高效率。

8. **竞争优势**：使组织超越竞争对手的特质。迈克尔·E.波特认为，竞争优势使得组织比竞争对手成本更低，或是提供竞争对手无法供

应但却有市场的差异化产品。

9. **竞争战略**：企业主可用来提高其业务盈利能力的手段。

10. **互补者**：波特的五力分析模型的许多延伸中，互补者销售的产品或服务是其他企业销售的产品或服务的补充。比如：打印机制造商和纸张制造商；杜松子酒制酒商和奎宁水装瓶公司。这个概念由商业学教授亚当·布兰登勃格首次提出。

11. **混合多元化战略**：企业通过增加新产品或服务，向与原业务无关的市场扩展。

12. **权变理论**：这一理论认为没有最好的管理方法，理想的管理取决于当前任务和环境，是多样化的。权变理论与韦伯的官僚制理论或泰勒的科学管理理论形成了对比，后两者都提出了单一的理想管理形式。

13. **企业社会责任**：最早在 20 世纪 60 年代流行的概念，认为公司有义务为其所在的社区和环境做贡献，并为股东创造价值。这可能包括支持慈善事业、购买"公平贸易"的材料和为减少废物和污染做贡献。

14. **成本与生产理论**：使用资源创造具有特定形式、数量和分配方式的合适商品或服务，这一生产过程创造出经济福祉。

15. **成本领先**：通过享有产业内最低的运营成本来取得竞争优势，方式有效率、规模、经验、技术、标准化产品及这些元素的组合，从而能够为客户提供最低价格。

16. **消费者行为**：对消费者及其决策过程（包括朋友和其他参考群体的影响）的研究。它将购买过程分解为认识问题、搜索信息、选择购买产品和实际购买产品。

17. **夕阳产业**：因产品需求下降而走入负增长或停滞不前的产业，即在一段时期内单位销售额持续下降的产业。

18. **金三角模型**：一种基于企业和客户关系，而不是竞争（比如波特的五力分析）的制定战略管理的方式。要点包括锁定客户以实现可持续盈利。该模型是由管理和战略学者迪恩·怀尔德和阿诺尔多·哈克斯开发的战略架构。

19. **解除管制**：在经济的所有领域中减少政府规定、限制或监管。解除管制是美国总统里根和英国首相撒切尔夫人经济政策的重要特征。

20. **差异化**：制造和同类产品不一样的产品。爱德华·张伯伦于 1933 年在《垄断竞争理论》一书中提出了该观点。差异化也是迈克尔·E. 波特的三种通用战略之一。

21. **互联网泡沫**：始于 1997 年的投机泡沫，2000 年 3 月达到顶峰，股价由于互联网行业的发展一路飙升。1999 到 2001 年间泡沫破裂，一些公司倒闭（比如 pet.com），另一些公司（比如 eBay 和 Amazon）市值暴跌，但随后又超过了泡沫时代的峰值。

22. **经济地理学**：针对经济活动地域的研究，包括解释产业集群出现的空间模型研究。知识、交通成本和正外部性的作用都是大多数相关研究中的重要概念，解释了为什么产业在某些地域发展得更快。

23. **规模经济**：在一定的产量范围内，随着产量的增加，平均成本不断降低。由于单位产出增加，固定成本（比如机械或建筑成本）不变，单位成本就随着规模增加而降低，从而企业获得成本优势。

24. **应急战略**：随着公司在经营中摸索出行之有效的方法，公司就会自然而然地形成战略。

25. **经验曲线**：观察发现，进行任务的次数越多，重复进行该任务所需时间就越少。从 1968 年开始，布鲁斯·亨德森和波士顿咨询集团就在宣传经验曲线对战略的影响。

26. **2008 年金融危机**：全球经济严重滑坡，世界范围内股价下跌，众多银行需要政府救济，世界各地失业率攀升，房地产市场下跌。2008 年金融危机是全球经济下滑的开端，这种经济衰退一直持续到 2012 年。

27. **五力和五力分析**：迈克尔·E. 波特提出的用来更好地理解市场竞争的框架。五种竞争因素包括新入市者、替代品的威胁、行业竞争程度、买方议价能力和供应商议价能力。根据五力分析模型，在

竞争相对不激烈的产业中更容易盈利。

28. **《财富》500强**：《财富》杂志每年根据企业收入评选的美国500强企业，1955年首次发布。

29. **四企业集中度**：衡量企业集中度的指标，即某一行业在多大程度上是寡头垄断的。它衡量的是行业内最大的四家企业的总市场份额。

30. **博弈论**：有关冲突与合作的数学模型，用于理解理性决策者的行为。20世纪40年代由数学家创立，如今是运用于经济学及社会科学的主要研究方法。

31. **通用电气**：美国跨国公司，由发明家托马斯·爱迪生于1892年创立，按收入计算常跻身《财富》500强中的美国10强企业榜单。该公司一半的收入来自金融服务，在能源和消费类电器行业也有大量业务。

32. **通用战略**：波特提出的三个选择，可让企业在其选择的市场中追求竞争优势。企业可以选择以最低的成本进行竞争，或者将自家产品与其他产品区分开来，或者可以专注于小众市场。

33. **全球化**：世界各国一体化的进程。交通和通讯的进步加快了全球化进程，思想、技术、商品的交换也越来越多。大规模的全球化始于19世纪的工业革命，之后全球化进程一直在加速。

34. **大萧条**：1929年开始，美国人民生活水平和就业率下降，并蔓延到世界各地，一直持续到20世纪30年代晚期。全球国内生产总值（GDP）从1929年到1932年下降了15%。美国的失业率上涨了25%。

35. **增长率**：一个经济体在一段时间内生产的产品和提供的服务经过通涨调整后计算得到的市场价值的增长。通常情况下，增长率以实际国内生产总值（GDP）的增长百分比来衡量。

36. **增长率—占有率矩阵**：布鲁斯·亨德森创立的波士顿咨询公司于1970年创建的图表，用于帮助企业分析其产品线。它根据企业的市场占有率和增长率来划分业务单元或产品，将其划分为现金牛业务、瘦狗型业务、问号型业务和明星型业务。

37. **赫芬达尔—赫希曼指数**：衡量企业在行业内的市场份额以及该行业内的竞争程度的指标。

38. **中区陷阱问题**：波特对"公司应该寻求更高市场份额"的观点提出的批评。他发现，低收入和高收入的公司都可能具有很高的盈利能力，而公司应该寻求的不是市场份额，而是盈利能力。收入处于中间的公司盈利能力最低。

39. **产业组织经济学**：研究公司和市场结构的经济学领域，关注阻碍完全竞争的复杂因素，如交易成本、有限的信息和新公司进入市场的壁垒。

40. **产业结构**：竞争同一业务的公司数量、客户和供应商数量、新入市者数量以及替代品的威胁。产业结构概念认为，企业的盈利能力取决于其所处的市场环境，而不仅仅取决于企业行为。

41. **勒纳指数**：衡量企业市场力量的指标，由俄罗斯裔英国经济学家阿巴·勒纳于 1934 年设计。它反映了企业提高商品或服务的市场价格以超过边际成本的能力。

42. **宏观经济学**：研究国家、地区和全球经济，以及国内生产总值、失业率和通货膨胀等指标的经济学分支。

43. **管理革命**：管理学学者、《管理革命》（1941）的作者詹姆斯·伯纳姆提出的概念。伯纳姆认为，管理者已经成为一个新的现代统治阶级，不受限制的资本主义正在被更有计划性、更集中的社会和经济所取代。

44. **边际成本**：多生产一件产品的额外成本。公司通过比较边际成本和销售价格来决定产品的产量。如果边际成本低于销售价格，公司将继续生产，直到两者相等为止。

45. **市场准入壁垒**：造成企业难以进入某一市场的障碍，可能是法规、知识产权（如专利）、许可和教育要求等，以及行业内领先企业享有的规模经济。

46. **市场准入**：企业进入新市场的过程。进入方式包括在新市场设立企业实体、直接出口、使用经销商或分销商、在目标市场生产产品。

47. **市场细分**：一种市场营销策略，将一个大的市场分割成具有共同需求的较小的客户群。

48. **市场份额**：某一特定企业在市场中所占的百分比（以单位或收入计算）。市场份额是市场竞争力的一个指标，可以衡量企业在与竞争对手的竞争中实力如何。

49. **市场规模**：一个市场中产品或服务的潜在买家或卖家的人数（或公司数量）。

50. **市场结构**：生产一种产品的公司的数量指标。在垄断的情况下，只有一家公司；在寡头垄断的情况下，有若干家公司。

51. **营销短视**：企业专注于销售产品而不是满足客户需求的错误。1960年，西奥多·莱维特在《哈佛商业评论》上发表了同名文章。

52. **大批量生产**：大量标准化商品的生产，尤指使用装配线完成的生产。在 19 世纪末的工业革命，尤其是在 1908 年亨利·福特率先大规模生产 T 型福特汽车之后，这一技术得到了广泛应用。

53. **微观经济学**：研究个人和企业及其决策的经济学分支。

54. **摩立特集团**：迈克尔·E.波特和五名哈佛商学院的同事于 1983 年创办的一家商业战略咨询公司。该公司在 2008 年经济危机中遭受重创，并于 2012 年底申请破产。德勤于 2013 年 1 月收购了该公司。

55. **垄断**：由一个供应商（通常是一家公司）控制一种商品或服务的供应，该商品或服务没有接近的替代品，因此该供应商可以将价格提高至远高于边际生产成本。这样的市场状况就是垄断。

56. **买方垄断**：买方只有一个而卖方很多的市场。因此，买方有很大的权力来确定价格。

57. **新古典经济学**：20 世纪的一套经济学方法，主要研究边际收益、效用最大化、均衡等概念。新古典经济学是研究当今全球经济的主要经济学形式。

58. **网络效应**：一种商品或服务的一位用户对该商品或服务相对于其他

用户的价值的影响。例如电话和社交网络：电话和社交网络越普及，那么购买电话和使用社交网络的用户数量就会越多。

59. **占领运动**：在全球许多城市举行的一系列相互关联的抗议活动，反对全球金融体系中的不公正行为。开始于 2011 年 9 月纽约的"占领华尔街"运动。

60. **寡头垄断**：只有少数企业销售产品的市场。市场上只有少数企业，它们可能会合谋抬高价格或降低风险；或者，企业间会展开更激烈的竞争。

61. **机会成本**：最佳替代方案的价值就是机会成本。例如，你等待客户服务所付出的成本与你的等待时间和单位时间工资水平相对应，这个机会成本表示如果你没有等待客户服务则可以赚到的钱。

62. **石油输出国组织**：拥有 13 个成员国的政府间组织，包括伊朗、伊拉克、科威特、利比亚、阿拉伯联合酋长国和沙特阿拉伯等。该组织成立于 1960 年 9 月。

63. **PEST 分析模型**：关注政治、经济、社会和技术因素对企业环境影响的框架。如果要涵盖法律因素，该模型会扩展为 SLEPT 分析；如果要涵盖法律和环境因素，该模型会扩展为 PESTLE 分析。

64. **波特假说**：迈克尔·E. 波特在 1995 年的一篇文章中提出，更严格的环境监管可能会给市场带来效率和创新，从而使市场更具竞争力。

65. **定位**：一个品牌相对于其竞争对手所占据的一部分市场。这在很大程度上是通过广告实现的，广告将产品或服务归为廉价或高档、入门级或高端产品，或宣传该品牌的特色，如品牌相较于竞争对手有何特别之处。

66. **价格弹性**：一种商品或服务的需求随价格变化而变化的程度。

67. **生产导向**：公司专注于它所生产的产品或服务；通常情况下，这与市场（优先）导向形成对比，后者关注客户需求。

68. **战略与绩效分析（PIMS）**：西德尼·舍福勒从 20 世纪 60 年代到

1983 年间开展的一项对 200 家公司中的 2 600 个业务单元的调查，该调查确定了 37 个能够带来商业成功的变量，包括强大的市场地位、高质量产品、低成本和市场增长。

69. **资源基础理论**：通过分析企业可支配的有形或无形资源来判断企业的竞争优势。要获得持久的竞争优势，企业的资源必须是有价值的、稀有的、难以复制的和不可替代的。

70. **瑞安航空**：成立于 1984 年的爱尔兰低成本航空公司，目前首席执行官为迈克尔·奥利里。按乘客数量计算，它是世界上最繁忙的航空公司。1997 年，在欧洲航空业解除管制的背景下，它开创了一种低成本的商业模式，并开创了在线订票和廉价旅行方式。

71. **谢尔曼法**：1890 年通过的反垄断法，允许美国联邦政府打击托拉斯和垄断，以促进竞争。

72. **斯坦福国际研究院**：斯坦福大学于 1946 年在加利福尼亚州成立的研究机构，旨在支持周边地区的经济发展。

73. **战略契合**：衡量企业结构和能力与外部环境匹配程度的指标。它与资源基础理论相关，将盈利能力、持久的竞争优势与企业资源和能力相联系。

74. **战略定位**：公司关于如何创造不同于竞争对手的价值的决策；通常情况下，这需要企业决定是否收取更高溢价、寻求更低成本。

75. **战略**：在不确定的情况下实现目标的计划。战略在 20 世纪 60 年代成为商业和管理学的一个主题。此前战略主要与外交、军事和海军事务有关。

76. **结构—行为—绩效模型**：产业组织经济学中的一种模型，由经济学家乔·贝恩提出。该模型研究市场结构如何影响企业绩效。

77. **替代品**：可用于替代的、更便宜的产品或服务。

78. **替代效应**：一种商品的价格变化所产生的影响。当商品价格上涨时，消费者会购买更多的低价商品、更少的高价商品。这样，消费者将用较便宜的商品替代价格上涨的商品。

79. **供应商**：提供公司运营所需资源的公司。例如，小麦农场是面粉制造商的供应商，磨坊是面包店的供应商。

80. **供求理论 / 供需理论**：在竞争条件下决定市场价格的经济模型。在市场上，商品价格维持在供求平衡点上。

81. **持续竞争优势**：难以被竞争对手复制或改进的长期优势，包括获得自然或人力资源的优越渠道或使公司免于竞争的市场准入壁垒。

82. **转换成本**：消费者或企业在改变供应商、产品或品牌时产生的成本。

83. **SWOT 分析法（态势分析法）**：一种分析企业优势、劣势、机会和威胁的方法。20 世纪 60 年代和 70 年代，斯坦福研究所和阿尔伯特·汉弗莱普及了这种分析法。

84. **价值链**：企业为生产产品或服务而进行的一系列分散的活动。价值链将公司的活动看作一系列过程——一些过程的产出是后面的过程的投入。迈克尔·E.波特在 1985 年《竞争优势》一书中提出了这个概念。

85. **价值体系**：价值体系的概念将价值链的概念扩展到公司之外，将公司供应商和公司产品买方的过程连接了起来。

86. **风险投资家**：专门为初创公司提供资金的投资者。

87. **垂直整合**：指某一商品或服务的供应链中每一阶段都由一家公司负责。美国实业家安德鲁·卡耐基的钢铁制造就是一个早期的例子。

88. **第二次世界大战**：1939 年至 1945 年的全球战争，直接牵涉到 30 个国家的 1 亿多人，造成 5 000 万至 8 500 万人死亡。二战造成的结果包括亚洲和非洲的非殖民化、美国和苏联在冷战中的对立以及欧洲内部的政治一体化。

89. **莱特-帕特森空军基地**：美国空军最大的基地之一，位于俄亥俄州代顿市。新研发飞机的试飞常在此进行。

90. **排外思维**：对外国或外来文化人群的憎恶或恐惧。

人名表

1. **亚历山大大帝**，即亚历山大三世（公元前 356 年—公元前 323 年），南欧马其顿王国国王（自公元前 336 年）、波斯帝国国王（自公元前 330 年）、埃及国王（自公元前 332 年），创建了许多城市并以自己的名字命名，例如埃及的亚历山大港。同时也为古希腊文化的传播做出了巨大贡献。哲学家亚里士多德曾是亚历山大大帝的老师。

2. **肯尼斯·安德鲁斯**（1916—2005），曾任教于哈佛商学院，与其同事阿尔弗雷德·D. 钱德勒都是商业战略理念的重要奠基者。安德鲁斯认为，管理者通过尊重下属来获得权威，而企业若想生存，则必须拥有效力（完成共同目标的能力）与效率（满足个人动机的能力）。

3. **乔·贝恩**（1912—1991），经济学家，任教于加利福尼亚大学伯克利分校，在产业组织学领域举足轻重。他提出了进入壁垒的概念来解释产业绩效，同时他也关注与产业集中化相关的问题。

4. **切斯特·伯纳德**（1886—1961），商业领域研究专家，著作有 1938 年出版的《经理人员的职能》。

5. **亚当·布兰登勃格**，1987 年至 2002 年任教于哈佛商学院，与拜瑞·内勒巴夫共同创作《合作竞争》（1996）一书，主要探讨公司之间可寻求合作而非竞争的情况。

6. **理查德·凯维斯**（1931 年生），哈佛大学经济学教授，主要研究产业组织理论。

7. **阿尔弗雷德·D. 钱德勒**（1918—2007），哈佛商学院商业史学家，因 1977 年出版《看得见的手——美国企业的管理革命》而获得普利策历史奖。其著作主要讨论商业战略理念。

8. **格里高利·戴斯**，得克萨斯州管理学家，曾在《管理学会评论》发表文章，主要讨论公司的创业行为和高效能之间的联系。

9. **拉里·唐斯**，美国作家、商业领域研究专家，因与梅振家共同创作的《打造顶尖企业的 12 项原则》（2008）一书而知名。

10. **亨利·福特**（1863—1947），美国实业家、汽车制造商，率先使用流水作业线并将汽车推广到中产阶级。

11. **万斯·弗瑞德**，俄克拉荷马州立大学里阿达创业学教授。

12. **威廉·加特纳**（1953 年生），美国加利福尼亚州千橡市加利福尼亚路德大学、丹麦哥本哈根商学院商业研究教授，创业学专家。

13. **彼得·戈尔斯基**，美国风险资本家、项目经理、业余作家。

14. **阿诺尔多·哈克斯**，麻省理工学院阿尔弗雷德·P. 斯隆名誉教授，研究方向为战略管理。2001 年与迪恩·怀尔德合著《金三角模型：在网络经济中探索发展和利润的新来源》。

15. **布鲁斯·亨德森**（1915—1992），1963 年创建了波士顿咨询公司并担任公司的总裁兼首席执行官，直至 1980 年。他将公司的重点放在了战略咨询上，对公司的影响是非常深远的。在波士顿咨询公司的这段时间，他极力推广了经验曲线概念和增长率—占有率矩阵概念。

16. **阿尔伯特·汉弗莱**（1926—2005），管理顾问、商业领域研究专家，在斯坦福研究所任职期间，他推广了 SWOT 分析法（即态势分析法）。

17. **金麟洙**，韩国高丽大学管理学教授。

18. **马克·克莱默**，在《哈佛商业评论》中多次与迈克尔·E. 波特合作，以其在共享价值领域的研究而闻名。

19. **保罗·劳伦斯**（1922—2011），哈佛商学院组织行为学教授，因与组织理论学家杰伊·洛希对复杂组织中的差异化和一体化进行研究而知名。

20. **西奥多·莱维特**（1925—2006），德裔经济学家，任职于哈佛商学院，因在《哈佛商业评论》中发表文章《营销短视症》（1960）以及推广全球化理念而知名。

21. 林允哲，韩国科学技术学院学者。

22. 杰伊·洛希（1932 年生），哈佛商学院组织理论学家，因其对权变理论的探索而知名。权变理论认为没有哪种领导方式是最佳的，选择领导方式时，必须将环境因素考虑在内，将尊重团队成员作为目标，提供充分结构化的任务并拥有必须的权威。

23. 琼·玛格雷塔，哈佛商学院战略与竞争力研究院高级助理，该研究院由迈克尔·E. 波特设立。此前，琼·玛格雷塔曾担任《哈佛商业评论》编辑以及贝恩公司顾问。2011 年，她写了一本关于波特的书——《竞争战略论：一本书读懂迈克尔·波特》。

24. 罗杰·马丁，多伦多大学罗特曼商学院院长。

25. 亚历山大·米勒，田纳西大学商业领域研究专家，发表了诸多著作，包括 1997 年出版的教科书《战略管理》。

26. 亨利·明茨伯格（1939 年生），加拿大学者，自 1968 年起在麦吉尔大学任教，是该校克莱格霍恩管理学教授。他研究商业经营策略，敢于质疑传统，积累了大量的管理实践以及管理咨询经验。他强调组织内产生的应急战略的重要性——这种战略与高管（通常在顾问的协助下）实施的预定战略相对。

27. 拜瑞·内勒巴夫，耶鲁管理学院米尔顿·斯坦巴赫管理学教授，研究经营策略与博弈论，与亚当·布兰登勃格共同著有《合作竞争》（1996），主要探讨公司之间可寻求合作而非竞争的情况。

28. 本杰明·欧维亚特，佐治亚州立大学管理学院副教授。

29. 马其顿国王腓力二世（公元前 382 年—公元前 336 年），从公元前 359 年起一直是古希腊马其顿王国的国王，直至其遭遇刺杀。在位期间，他极大地拓宽了马其顿王国的疆土。他是亚历山大大帝的父亲。

30. 大卫·李嘉图（1772—1823），英国经济学家，因其关于比较优势的著作而闻名，他认为一个国家应当专注于该国在国际上最具有竞争力的行业。在生命的最后四年，大卫·李嘉图成为一名改革派议员。

31. **西德尼·舍福勒**，营销分析师，战略与绩效分析（PIMS）研究项目的发起人之一，此项目于 20 世纪 60 年代开始于通用电器公司，主要研究部分企业比其他企业盈利更多的原因，研究人员通过对各公司的市场地位以及战略的分析对它们进行评估。

32. **赫伯特·西蒙**（1916—2001），美国学者，从事决策研究，1978 年获诺贝尔经济学奖，他的主要贡献在于对不确定环境中决策过程的探讨。

33. **马修·斯图尔特**（1963 年生），波士顿作家、哲学家，1988 年获得牛津大学博士学位，之后成为管理顾问，他以批判性角度将自己作为管理顾问的工作经验以及咨询行业的情况写进了著作《管理学神话：解读现代企业哲学》中，该书于 2009 年由 W. W. 诺顿出版社出版。

34. **弗雷德里克·温斯洛·泰勒**（1856—1915），最早的管理顾问之一，美国机械工程师，在其 1911 年的著作《科学管理原理》中，他试图利用工程领域的原则来提高行业效率。他也是"效率增进运动"即"泰勒主义"的先驱之一。

35. **马克·吐温**（1835—1910），美国作家萨缪尔·克莱门的笔名，著有《汤姆·索亚历险记》（1876）和《哈克贝利·费恩历险记》（1885）。肯尼斯·安德鲁斯以马克·吐温为题撰写了博士论文，后成为一名优秀的管理学家。

36. **伯格·沃纳菲尔特**（1951 年生），丹麦经济学家、管理学家，拥有麻省理工学院 JC 潘尼管理学教席，1984 年在一篇期刊文章中提出了"企业资源基础理论"。

37. **迪恩·怀尔德**，战略顾问，麻省理工学院斯隆管理学院决策学访问教授，与阿诺尔多·哈克斯合著《金三角模型：在网络经济中探索发展和利润的新来源》。

WAYS IN TO THE TEXT

- Michael E. Porter is an American professor at Harvard Business School; born in 1947 in the US state of Michigan, he grew up around the world on account of his father's military career.

- In *Competitive Strategy* (1980), Porter identified five forces of competition* in an industry: suppliers* (providers of materials required by a business), buyers (customers), substitutes* (roughly, cheaper alternatives to a product or service), potential entrants (possible newcomers to a specific market), and industry rivals.

- Not only has Porter's book shaped the thinking of corporate leaders for 30 years, it has also attracted interest from academics and members of the wider public keen to understand how successful businesses behave.

Who Is Michael E. Porter?

The author of *Competitive Strategy: Techniques for Analyzing Industries and Competitors* (1980), Michael E. Porter, was born in 1947 in the city of Ann Arbor in the US state of Michigan. His father was a career army officer, and Michael grew up in a number of countries where his father served. He studied aerospace (aviation) and mechanical engineering at Princeton University, graduating first in his class in 1969. From there he went to Harvard University, where he earned an MBA with high distinction from the Harvard Business School in 1971, and a PhD in business economics in 1973.

Porter's research has focused on competitive strategy* (the means available to the business owner or organization seeking to increase the profitability or success of the business or organization over others) and competitiveness. His interest in this subject began with his experience in sports—as a high school student he was one of the top baseball and football players in his state, and as an undergraduate he was one of the top American university golfers.[1]

After earning his PhD, Porter remained in the academic world, lecturing at the Harvard Business School. In 1980, he published the first edition of *Competitive Strategy*. It quickly became an influential business text, and an international best seller; by 2016, it had been translated into 19 languages and had been reprinted 63 times. The text serves as part of the core curriculum at Harvard Business School, as well as at almost every business school in the world.

Since 2001, Porter has directed the Institute for Strategy and Competitiveness at Harvard Business School. He is one of the most cited academics in business and economics.[2]

His later publications have expanded on the ideas put forward in *Competitive Strategy*. They look at competitiveness at the level of the nation and the relationship between competition and society.

Porter has also served as a consultant to American politicians at various levels, to governments around the world, and to a good many companies looking to put the ideas in *Competitive Strategy* into action. He has also followed his lifelong love of sport by advising the Boston Red Sox baseball team on competitive strategy. As a consultant he has been generally successful, though in 2012 the consulting firm he cofounded, Monitor Group, went into bankruptcy. Porter lives in Brookline, Massachusetts.

What Does *Competitive Strategy* Say?

Competitive Strategy provides businesses with a strong framework for thinking about how to compete in their industries. This framework expands on a journal article Porter had written in the *Harvard Business Review* in 1979.[3]

In the first section of *Competitive Strategy*, Porter describes the five forces of competition: suppliers, buyers, substitute products, potential entrants, and industry rivals. This framework offers powerful tools for understanding a competitive environment.[4] His main aim in the text, however, was to answer the question of how companies might best succeed against their competitors.

Porter's answer is that they do this either by being more efficient and cheaper, or by being different, better, or more relevant. For Porter, these are the only two ways to succeed.

According to Porter it is not only a business's competitors who can have an effect on its performance; environmental factors are crucially important. Buyers, sellers, companies not yet in the industry (but who might enter it), and other products are also important. This was new thinking, going against what had been generally believed among business scholars at the time. Management writers before Porter had concentrated on areas he considered less important such as expanding market share.

The airline industry offers a useful example of Porter's ideas. For instance, the Irish airline Ryanair* has opted to compete in the market by using cost leadership*—structuring the business around low overhead costs and cheap prices. On the other hand, a company can charge more by providing services or technological innovation its competitors do not; Singapore Airlines, for example, was the first airline to offer individual television screens for passengers flying economy. Finally, a company can operate effectively if it can find a niche market, such as providing private jets.

While Porter did not invent these ideas about competing effectively by providing a cheaper or differentiated product, he certainly thought about them in new, thorough ways, and provided a framework that was easy to apply to a broad range of actual business scenarios. He built on nineteenth-century economic ideas of comparative advantage,* according to which a company—or a country—focuses on producing what it can make most cheaply and efficiently. He took those ideas and applied them in a new, clear way that makes sense with regard to modern business problems.

Competitive Strategy examines how to apply this framework to many different business sectors. For Porter, industries can be fragmented, with different firms serving different parts of the market (the low-price mass market, and the expensive high-end market in clothing, for example) and he examines strategies that businesses can follow in emerging, mature, and declining markets. If we assume printing to be in decline, for example, there may still be a market in this industry for high-end goods and services such as luxury craft bookbinding or letterpress (an old-fashioned printing technique in which letters are "set" with moveable blocks).

Porter's research has inspired many others to look into features of competition. He built on his own work in *Competitive Strategy* with his 1985 book *Competitive Advantage: Creating and*

Sustaining Superior Performance, where he introduced new ideas like the value chain,* a way of looking at a business's production of goods or services by breaking it down into a number of separate steps.

Porter's clever understanding of five forces that broadly shape all kinds of business competition attracted many different readers, from economists to heads of corporations and the general public.

Why Does *Competitive Strategy* Matter?

Since its publication in 1980, *Competitive Strategy* has remained an important text. At business schools throughout the world, it has been used to train business leaders to understand competitive markets, and has been a basis of Harvard Business School's own course for new chief executives of Fortune 500* companies (the biggest American companies as compiled by the US magazine *Fortune*). It has been hailed as one of the most influential business and management books of the last four decades.[5]

The five-force analysis technique outlined in the work will help executives run their businesses with a clear strategic direction, prepared for the way their competitors are likely to act, and with a sound knowledge of how their industry is developing.

Business professionals using Porter's tools will be able to plan ahead as if they are playing chess, always thinking a few moves ahead of their opponents, rather than paying attention to short-term operational challenges only.

As well as providing general theories for analyzing competition, *Competitive Strategy* also provides businesses with concrete lessons. For example, companies that position themselves as a low-cost option in their industry protect themselves at once against all five of Porter's competitive forces. Firms that are neither the low-cost option, nor the differentiated one, can charge a premium, but can also be stuck in the middle, needing time and long effort to get out of a tricky position. Porter investigates this in what he calls the "hole in the middle problem."*

Competitive Strategy has received a number of prizes, including the Academy of Management's award for outstanding contribution to management thought. Four different "Porter prizes" have since been named after the author, awarded to companies that have applied his lessons in an exemplary way in their industry— in Japan (2001), India (2012), South Korea (2014) and, more generally, health care (2014).[6]

Decades after publication, *Competitive Strategy* is still required reading for anyone interested in understanding how companies form strategies about how best to compete. As the dean of the University of Toronto's Rotman School of Business, Roger Martin* noted, "Everyone who talks about sustainable competitive advantage* and how they're going to get it [uses business concepts originated by Porter's *Competitive Strategy*.]"[7]

---

1. Walter Kiechel, *The Lords of Strategy: The Secret Intellectual History of the New Corporate World* (Cambridge, MA: Harvard Business Press, 2010).

2. Joan Magretta, *Understanding Michael Porter: The Essential Guide to Competition and Strategy* (Cambridge, MA: Harvard Business Review Press, 2011).

3. Michael E. Porter, "How Competitive Forces Shape Strategy," *Harvard Business Review* 57.2 (1979): 86–93.

4. Michael E. Porter, *Competitive Strategy: Techniques for Analyzing Industries and Competitors*, 2nd ed. (New York: Free Press, 1998).

5. Arthur Bedeian and Daniel Wren, "Most Influential Management Books of the 20th Century," *Organizational Dynamics* 29.3 (2001): 221–25.

6. The Porter Prize, "About," accessed January 29, 2016, http://www.porterprize.org/english/about/.

7. Geoff Colvin, "There's No Quit in Michael Porter," *Fortune Magazine*, October 15, 2012, accessed January 29, 2016, http://fortune.com/2012/10/15/theres-no-quit-in-michael-porter/.

SECTION 1
INFLUENCES

THE AUTHOR AND THE HISTORICAL CONTEXT

KEY POINTS

- *Competitive Strategy* introduced new ways of considering strategy—plans to achieve certain goals—and competition* in the business sector.

- Porter's childhood interest in competitive sport inspired his interest in strategic approaches to competition.

- In the years since *Competitive Strategy* was written, nearly every business school graduate has been exposed to the principles in Porter's book, giving it a tremendous influence on the business sector as a whole.

Why Read This Text?

Michael E. Porter's *Competitive Strategy: Techniques for Analyzing Industries and Competitors* (1980) is one of the most important texts in the field of business management and strategy. According to Joan Magretta,* a well-known former editor of the leading business magazine *Harvard Business Review*, Porter is "the most cited scholar in economics and business. At the same time, his ideas are the most widely used in practice by business and government leaders around the world. His frameworks have become the foundation of the strategy* field."[1]

Competitive Strategy introduces several key concepts, notably the five forces* of suppliers* (those who provide the resources and services a business requires), buyers (customers), substitutes* (less expensive replacements for a product or service), potential entrants (newcomers to a specific market), and industry rivals. Others were competitive advantage* (qualities that allow an organization to outperform competitors), the value chain* (the various activities a business performs to produce a good or service), industry structure* (the nature of the business environment), and differentiation* (making a product different to others on the market).

Today, these ideas are used widely, but not always as Porter had intended—many refer to these concepts according to an inaccurate or incomplete understanding.[2] To understand the work's powerful insights and put them into practice requires that we are aware of and avoid frequent misunderstandings.

There is a misconception that competition is about being the best; for Porter, it is about being unique. Many wrongly think competition is a contest to the death between rivals—actually, it is strictly a battle over profits. And while many think strategy means being all things to all people, it requires, in fact, choices to make some customers happy.[3] The sign of a good strategy, according to Porter, is that it deliberately makes some customers unhappy.

> *"It is hard to concoct a logic in which the nature of the arena in which firms compete would not be important to performance outcomes."*
>
> —— Michael E. Porter, *Competitive Strategy: Techniques for Analyzing Industries and Competitors*

Author's Life

Born in 1947 into an army family in Michigan, Porter travelled widely abroad throughout his childhood, experiencing different countries and cultures. On returning to the United States, he excelled in competitive sports—baseball, football, and golf—in both secondary school and university, which further increased his interest in competition and strategy.

Academically, he began as a student of engineering, graduating from Princeton University in 1969. He then adapted his technical and mathematical background to business and economics. Immediately after graduating, he went to Harvard University for a Master of Business Administration degree (MBA) and then moved on to the graduate school, where he completed a doctorate in business economics in 1973.

Porter is best known for work on competitiveness and strategy, which he brought together in his 1980 book *Competitive Strategy*. He first began exploring the ideas in the book in an academic article on the subject in the *Harvard Business Review*, published the year before.[4] He then continued to expand on the ideas in *Competitive Strategy* in other books, notably *Competitive Advantage: Creating and Sustaining Superior Performance* (1985). In total, he has written 19 books, and is widely considered the father of the modern strategy field.[5] He holds the chair of Bishop William Lawrence University Professor at the Harvard Business School, one of the 24 most senior professorial posts in the university.

In 2000, Harvard established an Institute for Strategy and Competitiveness, based in the Harvard Business School, whose website describes its mission as "extending the research pioneered by Porter and disseminating it to scholars and practitioners on a global basis."⁶ The institute focuses on competition and its implications for company strategy; on the competitiveness of larger units than companies, such as nations, regions, and cities; and on the relationship between competition and society.

Author's Background

Porter's early work pioneered the use of economic theory to understand in a more thorough way the choices companies make to compete, and the dynamics of competition within an industry. The two most important themes in *Competitive Strategy* are industry structure (the make-up of the market place in terms of businesses, customers, products, and so on) and strategic positioning* (the means available to a business to place itself in the market in the most beneficial way). Along with his later idea of the value chain (the activities performed by a business as it brings a product to market) these remain central to Porter's work.

The 1980s in the United States were a time of both economic expansion and insecurity about the rise of competition from East Asian companies, especially from Japan. *Competitive Strategy* offered American businesses an intellectual framework for planning to compete with Japanese companies.

After writing *Competitive Strategy*, Porter further explored its ideas by turning to economic development and competitiveness on bigger scales—that is to say, he used microeconomic* factors (economics on a smaller scale—decisions of a single company, for example) to study the economic development of regions and nations. Here, he developed the idea of clusters* and created the Cluster Mapping Project,* which studies clusters of related business in US regions. He helped pioneer the field of economic geography*—a field that looks to map how transport costs and closeness to suppliers, personnel, and other businesses make some industries develop in some places quicker than in others.

Other areas in which Porter went on to apply the ideas in *Competitive Strategy* include health care and the role of corporations in society. His work—especially a 2011 article coauthored with the business strategist Mark Kramer,* "Creating Shared Value"[7]—has helped change the way companies approach corporate social responsibility;* Porter describes corporate social responsibility not as philanthropy (giving money to others), but as creating social value by, for example, locating business projects and enterprises in places that will help poor people.

Porter is also well known for the "Porter hypothesis,"* which holds that strict environmental standards could improve both company profits and national competitiveness by encouraging innovation and efficiency. This hypothesis has prompted several hundred academic articles by other scholars in the field of environmental economics.[8]

Indeed, a senior editor at *Fortune* magazine said of Porter: "He has influenced more executives—and more nations—than any other business professor on earth."[9]

---

1. Joan Magretta, *Understanding Michael Porter: The Essential Guide to Competition and Strategy* (Cambridge, MA: Harvard Business Review Press, 2011).

2. See Magretta, *Understanding Michael Porter*, 121–40.

3. Magretta, *Understanding Michael Porter*, 111.

4. Michael E. Porter, "How Competitive Forces Shape Strategy," *Harvard Business Review* 57.2 (1979): 86–93.

5. Antonio Nieto-Rodriguez, *The Focused Organization: How Concentrating on a Few Key Initiatives Can Dramatically Improve Strategy Execution* (Burlington, VT: Ashgate, 2012), 202.

6. Institute for Strategy and Competitiveness, "Home," accessed January 29, 2016, http://www.isc.hbs.edu/.

7. Michael E. Porter and Mark R. Kramer, "Creating Shared Value," *Harvard Business Review*, (2011): 63–70.

8. Google Scholar, "Porter Hypothesis," accessed January 29, 2016, https://scholar.google.com/scholar?hl=en&q=%22Porter+Hypothesis%22&btnG=&as_sdt=1%2C9&as_sdtp=.

9. Geoff Colvin, "There's No Quit in Michael Porter," *Fortune Magazine*, October 15, 2012, accessed January 29, 2016, http://fortune.com/2012/10/15/theres-no-quit-in-michael-porter/.

ACADEMIC CONTEXT

KEY POINTS

* Strategy began with military campaigns and national government; it entered the business vocabulary after World War II* (1939–45).

* Academics including Kenneth Andrews* at the Harvard Business School adapted the concept of strategy to business so that it could be taught to business students.

* *Competitive Strategy* was written toward the end of a century that saw a number of great management experts who looked at different issues in running a successful company.

The Work in Its Context

In *Competitive Strategy: Techniques for Analyzing Industries and Competitors*, Michael E. Porter describes strategy* as a "broad formula for how a business is going to compete, what its goals should be, and what policies will be needed to carry out those goals."[1] For him, it is the "combination of the ends (goals) for which the firm is striving and the means (policies) by which it is seeking to get there."[2]

One of Porter's key findings about business strategy is the claim that companies should specialize in a particular section of their market, rather than try to be all things to all people. This reflects ideas of comparative advantage* that trace back to the economist David Ricardo* in the nineteenth century. According to Ricardo, each country should practice extreme specialization in the industries in which it is most competitive. For example, member nations of the Organization of Petroleum Exporting Countries* (OPEC) specialize in crude oil production, and Canada specializes in maple syrup (among many other products).

Producing any products other than the ones that it can produce at the lowest marginal cost* ("products A") means a country must pay the opportunity cost* of producing other commodities ("products B"), when it could have been producing products A instead. "Marginal cost" here is the extra cost of producing one more unit; "opportunity cost" is the value of the best alternative action to the one actually taken.

If a country uses its resources to produce more of product A, it can sell the excess and use the revenue to buy product B from a nation that can produce product B most efficiently. For example, Iceland has a large and efficient fisheries industry. It exports large quantities of cod and uses the earnings to buy many things it cannot produce efficiently, such as bananas. This is a wise choice, since if Iceland decided instead to take some investment capital and workers away from the fisheries to build and use expensive heated hot houses to grow bananas, it would end up with fewer cod to sell and fewer bananas to eat.

Ricardo's work on comparative advantage is actually the basis for the widespread present-day agreement in favor of free trade. If each country focuses on producing products that it makes best, by selling those products to other countries it can generate income with which to purchase items that it is less efficient at producing— and at a greater volume than it could have made on its own.

In *Competitive Strategy*, Porter argues that companies should focus sharply on a particular niche, like resource extraction (mining minerals or extracting oil, for example), manufacturing certain goods, or providing certain services.

> *"A number of other books about competition have come and gone because they were really about special cases, or were grounded not in the principles of competitive strategy but in particular competitive practices."*
>
> ——Michael E. Porter, *Competitive Strategy: Techniques for Analyzing Industries and Competitors*

Overview of the Field

The notion of strategy has been around since perhaps even the dawn of nation states. Leaders use strategies (the plan) and tactics (the maneuvers) to ensure victory over an opponent. The term derives from the Greek word for generalship, *stratēgia.* A *stratēgos* is a general, and this was the title of the fourth-century B.C.E. military leader and conqueror Alexander the Great* and his father, Philip II of Macedon.* Over time, the field of strategic studies has grown up. This includes military strategy and business strategy and any other field where there is a degree of competition.*

However, the shift from military to business strategy did not take place until after World War II. The business strategist Kenneth Andrews played a key role. In 1946, he joined the Harvard Business School faculty after earning a doctorate on the famous American writer Mark Twain* and serving in the army during the war. In 1950, he and several colleagues began revising the school's business policy course. After two years, they selected the concept of corporate strategy as the course's organizing principle.

Andrews began writing case studies (studies of real-life examples) from the point of view of senior management, specifically addressing all of the challenges facing a company such as the identification of threats and opportunities, and understanding what the company stands for. The course produced two important books: *Business Policy: Text and Cases* (1965), and *The Concept of Corporate Strategy* (1971).[3]

In Andrews's early formulation of business strategy, strategy was deliberate—consciously decided and adopted by management. His principles included that strategies must have an ethical component, and that they must be in agreement with the values of the upper managers.

A different view was advanced by Henry Mintzberg,* a Canadian academic business strategist for whom the approach was undemocratic and too "top-down" (that is, focused on management). He instead emphasized the importance of what he called "emergent strategy"*—strategy that emerges informally at any level in an organization. It is an alternative to, or a supplement for, the deliberate strategy determined by, or with the agreement of, senior management.

Academic Influences

By the time Porter had developed the ideas in *Competitive Strategy*, the book included ideas contributed by other colleagues, too. The business historian Alfred DuPont Chandler,* who came to the Harvard Business School in 1970, received a Pulitzer prize (a prestigious literary prize) in 1977 for his book *The Visible Hand: The Managerial Revolution in American Business*.[4] Chandler's book formed part of a "managerial revolution"* that looked at the importance of managers in organizing and running large businesses.

Chandler had also written an earlier book, *Strategy and Structure: Chapters in the History of the American Industrial Enterprise* (1962), which looked at large American businesses, tracing how each company's business strategy determined how the company was structured.[5] Chandler summarized his argument with the phrase "Structure follows strategy."[6]

Other academics promptly turned this around, suggesting strategy follows structure. A multidivision structure (in which a company is divided into different divisions strongly separated from one another), for example, leads a business to adopt a conglomerate strategy,*[7] in which it adds new goods or services to diversify into different markets unrelated to its current business.

It is worth placing *Competitive Strategy* in context alongside the other chief management books of the twentieth century. The first and most influential remains the early management scholar Frederick Winslow Taylor's* *The Principles of Scientific Management* (1911).[8] Taylor advocated running a business in the most efficient way with workplace tasks standardized so that they might be performed in the shortest amount of time. The book led to the start of management as a discipline.

The business scholar Chester Barnard's* *The Functions of*

the Executive (1938),[9] was the next, and one of the first books to consider leadership from a social and psychological viewpoint (that is, considering the role of the human mind in behavior). Herbert Simon's* suitably titled *Administrative Behavior: A Study of Decision-Making Processes in Administrative Organizations* (1947) remains one of the most cited management works in social science.[10]

A skeptical note came in with the influential management scholars Paul Lawrence* and Jay Lorsch's* *Organization and Environment* in 1967,[11] which questioned whether there was a single best way to organize, independent of the details of the industry, market, or overall business environment. Lawrence and Lorsch did not believe there was, and instead introduced the concept of contingency,* according to which ideal leadership differs based on the task and environment.

Competitive Strategy draws on a tradition of business strategy that had begun to flourish at the Harvard Business School in the years before Porter began working there. However, where earlier writers focused on ethics or efficiency, Porter turns the discussion about strategy to the conflict of companies with one another in the marketplace.

1. Michael E. Porter, *Competitive Strategy: Techniques for Analyzing Industries and Competitors*, 2nd ed. (New York: Free Press, 1998), xxiv.

2. Porter, *Competitive Strategy*, xxiv.

3. Philip Learned et al., *Business Policy: Text and Cases* (Homewood, IL: R. D. Irwin, 1969); and

Kenneth R. Andrews, *The Concept of Corporate Strategy* (Homewood, IL: R. D. Irwin, 1994).

4. Alfred Chandler, *The Visible Hand: The Managerial Revolution in American Business* (Cambridge, MA: Belknap Press, 1977).

5. Alfred Chandler, *Strategy and Structure: Chapters in the History of the American Industrial Enterprise* (Cambridge, MA: MIT Press, 1962).

6. Chandler, *Strategy and Structure*, 14.

7. David Hall and Maurice Saias, "Strategy Follows Structure!" *Strategic Management Journal* 1.2 (1980): 149–63.

8. Frederick Winslow Taylor, *The Principles of Scientific Management* (New York: Harper Brothers, 1911).

9. Chester Barnard, *The Functions of the Executive* (Cambridge, MA: Harvard University Press, 1938).

10. Herbert Simon, *Administrative Behavior: A Study of Decision-Making Processes in Administrative Organizations* (New York: Macmillan, 1947).

11. Paul Lawrence and Jay Lorsch, *Organization and Environment* (Boston, MA: Harvard Business School, Division of Research,1967).

MODULE 3
THE PROBLEM

KEY POINTS

* Through the mid-1950s, companies focused on increasing production to increase profit; with growing consumer choice, however, Porter proposed instead a focus on better satisfying consumers in a section of the market.

* As Porter developed his ideas in the 1970s, he drew on several leading, competing, models of business strategy.

* Finding problems with all the leading models, Porter ended up drawing most from the economist Joe Bain's* structure-conduct-performance* model, which looks at how market structure affects a business's performance.

Core Question

In *Competitive Strategy: Techniques for Analyzing Industries and Competitors*, Michael E. Porter asks how companies can best find profitable industries to compete in, and, having found an attractive industry, what strategy they should adopt to compete most effectively.

He poses the question of how companies should make important choices about the scope and type of competitive advantage*— qualities that permit an organization to outperform competitors— they seek in their industries. According to earlier studies, business strategies should simply be aimed at selling the highest volume of products possible.[1] Porter found this answer unsatisfying; more, it was not in keeping with empirical (real-world) research into which companies made the largest profits and competed most effectively.

Throughout the mid-1950s, a production orientation* strategy was most common in industry; this presumed that if a company created a long-lasting product of high technical quality that worked well, it would return a profit.

The Harvard Business School professor Theodore Levitt* helped replace this production orientation model in an important 1960 *Harvard Business Review* article called "Marketing Myopia."* He called on companies to switch to a consumer orientation by working to meet customers' needs, rather than start with a superior product and then think of how to sell it.[2]

A perfect example of this is when Henry Ford,* the founder of the Ford Motor Company, mockingly said customers could have a Model T (the first mass-produced, and relatively affordable car) in any color they liked, so long as it was black.[3] At the time of his comment, however, there had been a shortage of consumer goods that would worsen during the catastrophic economic downturn of the late 1920s and 1930s, known as the Great Depression,* and World War II* (1939–45), which meant that businesses only needed to produce a technically superb product to find a market.

Levitt's new consumer orientation model appeared to be better suited to an era of economic growth, when a growing supply of consumer goods was available. However, this model required the adoption of a new set of tools that business leaders could use to make strategic business decisions that took into account broader issues, like rival producers and customers faced with a variety of choices. It is these tools that Porter tries to provide in *Competitive Strategy*.

> "The essence of formulating competitive strategy is relating
> a company to its environment ... [The] key aspect of the firm's
> environment is the industry or industries in which it competes.
> The intensity of competition in an industry is neither a
> matter of coincidence nor bad luck. Rather, competition in an
> industry is rooted in its underlying economic structure and
> goes well beyond the behavior of current competitors."
>
> —— Michael E. Porter, *Competitive Strategy:
> Techniques for Analyzing Industries and Competitors*

The Participants

A scholar who made a significant contribution to this debate was
Albert Humphrey* of Stanford Research International,* a research
institute of Stanford University in California, who in the 1960s and
1970s helped popularize the so-called SWOT analysis,* studying
Strengths, Weaknesses, Opportunities, and Threats, to help a
business against its competitors. Humphrey considered a business
to have a strategic fit*—a suitable place in the market—if its
resources and capabilities matched with opportunities in its external
environment.

A second important scholar was Bruce Henderson,* founder
of the Boston Consulting Group,* a leading management consulting
firm. Beginning in 1968, he began drawing lessons for strategy
from what scholars call the "experience curve."* This curve reflects
the idea that the more often you do something, the more easily and
efficiently you can do it again. It was first measured in 1936 at
Wright-Patterson Air Force Base* in Dayton, Ohio, where it was

recognized that when work on aircraft doubled, the required labor time decreased 10–15 percent; in other industries, this was as high as 30 percent.

Henderson concluded that a lower cost of operations gives a company an important advantage over competitors. Therefore, businesses should focus on getting enough market share*—the percentage of a market accounted for by a particular business—to take advantage of the experience curve. For Henderson, producing more of an item gives employees more experience in producing it—and an advantage over rivals.

A third key scholar was Joe Bain, an important figure in industrial organization economics.* Bain focused not on businesses or the economy as a whole, but on a particular industry. Looking into questions such as barriers to entering a specific industry, he developed what was called the structure-conduct-performance paradigm, which considers how market structure—the "environment" of competition, customer base, products, and so on—affects a business's performance.[4]

A fourth scholar, who like Bain had an important influence on Porter, was Alfred DuPont Chandler,* a colleague at the Harvard Business School who won a Pulitzer prize for his book *The Visible Hand: The Managerial Revolution in American Business* three years before Porter's *Competitive Strategy* was published.

The Contemporary Debate

Before *Competitive Strategy* appeared, the leading view in business strategy was derived from the analysis of Bruce Henderson;

companies were encouraged to try to gain the highest market share to take advantage of the experience curve.

But this approach found challenges. In the late 1960s, the marketing analyst Sidney Schoeffler* of the US business giant General Electric* began a large research project, the Profit Impact of Marketing Strategy (PIMS),* which collected observations from 2,600 business units in 200 companies between 1970 and 1983. In contrast to Henderson's views on strategy, not only were firms with a high market share often very profitable, so were firms with *low* market share. The least profitable firms fell in the middle, with moderate market share—a "hole in the middle"* problem.[5] Porter also found that Henderson's SWOT analysis was not sufficiently thorough; he turned instead to the recent work of the economist Joe Bain for a model.

Bain's structure-conduct-performance model (on which Porter bases his own five forces)* looks for relationships between the structure of a market and an industry's performance. In particular, it looks for connections between how businesses behave in an industry, and the structure of the surrounding market—the barriers to new companies entering, how different are the products of different companies, and the degree to which supply and demand is concentrated in a particular region or section of the population.

Also at around this time, Chandler's *Visible Hand* had drawn great attention to the importance of a team of managers in organizing complex modern businesses.[6] But Chandler's book was a work of economic history rather than business strategy, and it reinforced in the public mind—and in Porter's—the importance of providing career business administrators with professional technical skills for their job.

1. *The Economist* editors, "The Experience Curve," *The Economist*, September 14, 2009, accessed February 8, 2016, http://www.economist.com/node/14298944.
2. Theodore Levitt, "Marketing Myopia," *Harvard Business Review* (1960): 45–56.
3. Henry Ford with Samuel Crowther, *My Life and Work* (Garden City, NY: Doubleday, Page, 1923), 72.
4. Joseph S. Bain, *Industrial Organization* (New York: John Wiley & Sons, 1959).
5. Michael E. Porter, *Competitive Strategy: Techniques for Analyzing Industries and Competitors*, 2nd ed. (New York: Free Press, 1998), 42.
6. Alfred Chandler, *The Visible Hand: The Managerial Revolution in American Business* (Cambridge, MA: Belknap Press, 1977).

MODULE 4
THE AUTHOR'S CONTRIBUTION

KEY POINTS

* In *Competitive Strategy*, Porter offers a model of competitive forces in an industry and how these forces affect the profitability of businesses competing in it.

* Porter's five forces* include three "horizontal" forces (established rivals, new entrants, and the threat of substitute products) and two "vertical" forces (the bargaining power of suppliers,* on one side, and consumers on the other).

* Other strategy planning tools for businesses include Bruce Henderson's* somewhat superseded growth-share matrix,* focusing on market share, and the political, economic, social, and technological PEST analysis,* often seen today along with Porter's five forces.

Author's Aims

In *Competitive Strategy: Techniques for Analyzing Industries and Competitors*, Michael E. Porter tries to use recent research to take a broader view of all the forces impacting on a business. As Porter says, "competition* in an industry goes well beyond the established players. Customers, suppliers, substitutes,* and potential entrants are all 'competitors' to firms in the industry and may be more or less prominent depending on the particular circumstances."[1]

By using a framework that takes each of these into account, managers and strategists can make better-informed decisions about which markets to compete in, and how to go about it.

Porter published *Competitive Strategy* in 1980. He had been lecturing at the Harvard Business School since completing his doctorate in business economics in 1973. He was influenced by coursework in industrial organization economics* (inquiry into the structure of firms and markets) that he took there as a student. This coursework attempted to model how competitive forces affected industries and how profitable the industries were in different circumstances.

During the 1960s and 1970s, researchers at the Harvard Business School such as Kenneth Andrews* and Alfred DuPont Chandler* had been looking into the drivers of profitability. The research had led these and other scholars to become particularly interested in the problems of strategy and the role of senior managers.

Yet two leading approaches to analyzing problems of strategy for managers—the Strengths, Weaknesses, Opportunities, and Threats (SWOT) analysis* and the experience curve,* founded on the observation that the more times a task has been performed, the less time is required to perform it again—struck Porter as flawed. The SWOT analysis, though still frequently used today, was not based on any thorough research or theory, and the experience curve did not explain how businesses with a small market share* (a percentage of the market) could be equally profitable to ones with very large shares.

> *"The collective strength of these [five basic competitive] forces determines the ultimate profit potential in the industry, where profit potential is measured in terms of long run return on invested capital. Not all industries have the same potential."*
>
> —— Michael E. Porter, *Competitive Strategy: Techniques for Analyzing Industries and Competitors*

Approach

Porter's five forces* sum up how competitive and attractive an industry is by looking at what affects the ability of a business in that industry to make a profit.

The five forces Porter identified are:

- the bargaining power of suppliers (those who supply things such as materials to a business)
- the threat of established rivals
- the threat of new entrants (newcomers to a market)
- the bargaining power of buyers (that is, roughly, consumer choice)
- the threat of substitution.

A business within an industry can then make profits that are more or less than the industry average by coming up with a business model that is better or worse than its competitors.

Porter also tackles the hole in the middle problem*—why, in the experience curve model, firms with very small or very large market share are successful, while ones in the middle are less profitable.

Porter argues that high market-share businesses follow a strategy of cost leadership: * using mass production* (mechanized production on a large scale) and taking advantage of economies of scale* (the fact that it is cheaper, per unit, to produce goods in greater quantities), they are able to offer a product more cheaply than their competitors. Small market-share businesses instead successfully use a strategy of market segmentation: * they correctly identify a niche in the market that is small but profitable.

Firms with a market share in the middle, on the other hand, are less likely to be able to compete with larger firms on cost, or with smaller firms in satisfying the needs of a niche. They are the least profitable as a result.

Contribution in Context

The five-forces approach Porter outlined in *Competitive Strategy* is one of several widely used analyses for understanding how to compete within a given industry.

An older approach, developed by Bruce Henderson* at the Boston Consulting Group* in 1970, is called the growth-share matrix.* Also known as "the product portfolio" or "portfolio planning analysis," it ranks business units or products based on their market share and growth rate. "Cash cows" have high market share in a slow-growing industry (and are to be milked, with low investment), whereas "dogs" have low market share in a slow-growing industry (and are to be sold off). "Stars" command high market share in a fast-growing industry, and require high funding to fight off competition, while "question marks" have low market share in a high-growth market, and will evolve into one of the other three.

One drawback of this approach is that it charts market share and an industry's growth rate, and only *suggests* profitability—the actual purpose of any business. Moreover, research has shown that businesses using this approach had lower shareholder returns than ones that did not.[2] Many business textbooks have begun removing the growth-share matrix.

Another framework for strategic analysis in looking at different factors in a company's environment is the PEST analysis, named for its analysis of political, economic, social, and technological factors. Political factors include tax policy; economic factors include interest rates; social factors include how quickly consumers within an economy are aging; technological factors include the rate of technological change. It should be noted that there are variants of this; with legal factors included, it is known as the "SLEPT" analysis; with environmental and legal factors it becomes a "PESTLE" framework.

---

1. Michael E. Porter, *Competitive Strategy: Techniques for Analyzing Industries and Competitors*, 2nd ed. (New York: Free Press, 1998), 6.
2. Stanley Slater and Thomas Zwirlein, "Shareholder Value and Investment Strategy Using the General Portfolio Model," *Journal of Management* 18.4 (1992): 717–32.

SECTION 2
IDEAS

MAIN IDEAS

KEY POINTS

* Porter says businesses should look at five key issues in their particular industry: the threat of new entrants; the threat of substitute products; the power of buyers; the power of suppliers;* industry rivals.
* For Porter, who looks at each of these competitive forces in detail, strategy is principally a question of building and sustaining competitive advantage.*
* The language used by Porter in *Competitive Strategy* is directed at business practitioners, and is remarkably free of jargon, academic language, or mathematics.

Key Themes

The core themes of Michael E. Porter's *Competitive Strategy: Techniques for Analyzing Industries and Competitors* are the effects on competition* of new entrants, substitute products, buyer power, supplier power, and the intensity of industry rivalry.

New entrants are businesses that are not currently present in a sector. However, they may see profitable markets, and will tend to enter them until—due to the increased competition—the profitability has decreased for all businesses in the sector.

Substitute products are goods that a consumer sees as similar or comparable. While, for the beverage producer Coke, Pepsi is a competitor for shares in the soft-drink market, the soft-drink market itself grows or shrinks as people choose instead to drink coffee drinks, energy drinks, alcoholic beverages, or sparkling water.

These are substitute products.

Buyer power is the bargaining ability of customers. It is high if buyers have many alternatives, or if there are only a few large buyers, or if buyers organize together to bargain. On the other hand, it is low if a large number of small buyers act independently of each other. An example of strong buyer power is Groupon, an online business that negotiates deals with other businesses for lower prices for Groupon clients, because of their large numbers. An extreme case is monopsony*—a situation where there is only one buyer in a market. The National Health Service in the United Kingdom is close to this, being practically the sole purchaser of hospital equipment in the country, and so can negotiate better deals. This is unlike in the United States, where each hospital has to purchase equipment independently.

Supplier power is closely related, and is the bargaining power of companies selling the materials and equipment that other producers need. An example of high supplier power is if a company bakes bread and there is only one firm selling flour—the company has no choice but to buy it. If there are many suppliers of flour, the baking business can hold out for a lower price.

Finally, industry rivalry reflects how aggressively competitors in a sector apply pressure to one another, and attempt to steal other businesses' market share and profits. Rivalry is high if there are many competitors, if they are of comparable market share, if brand loyalty is low, and if their products are undifferentiated (that is, can easily be substituted for one another). If an industry is growing quickly, or if the switching costs* to customers are high (that is, if it is costly for customers to switch to another producer, perhaps because customers have already invested in equipment to use the original product, and the equipment cannot be used for a competitor's product), then the industry rivalry may be low.

> "The goal of competitive strategy for a business unit in an industry is to find a position in the industry where the company can best defend itself against these competitive forces or can influence them in its favor. Since the collective strength of the forces may well be painfully apparent to all competitors, the key for developing strategy is to delve below the surface and analyze the sources of each."
>
> —— Michael E. Porter, *Competitive Strategy: Techniques for Analyzing Industries and Competitors*

Exploring the Ideas

Porter deals with each of the competitive forces one by one. "New entrants to an industry," writes Porter, "bring new capacity, the desire to gain market share, and often substantial resources."[1] Therefore they can bid down prices, and reduce profitability for businesses already in the sector. On the other hand, Porter believes that outside firms could be discouraged from entering a sector by the economies of scale* (the lower cost per item that often comes from producing a large quantity of that item) enjoyed by companies that already have more market share, or the need to differentiate themselves, "forcing entrants," in Porter's words, "to spend heavily to overcome existing customer loyalties," which "usually involves start-up losses and often takes an extended period of time."[2]

Second is the threat of substitute products. Porter argues they "limit the potential returns of an industry by placing a ceiling on the prices firms in the industry can profitably charge."[3] For example, sugar producers may find a lid set on their profits by a low price for high fructose corn syrup, a substitute for sugar. Other forces, like switching costs (moving from one product to another), may help reduce the threat.

Third is buyers' bargaining power. Companies in an industry do not only compete with each other—they also compete with buyers, by "forcing down prices, bargaining for higher quality or more services, and playing competitors against each other—all at the expense of industry profitability," Porter notes.[4] One strategic decision, therefore, is which buyers a company chooses to sell to. "A company can improve its strategic posture by finding buyers who possess the least power to influence it adversely," Porter says.[5]

The fourth is supplier power. Suppliers can threaten to raise prices or reduce the quality of the goods or services they offer. An industry unable to pass on price increases to customers will see its profitability squeezed out. Labor, for Porter, is a supplier: "Highly skilled employees and/or tightly unionized labor [workers organized with the aim of protecting things such as pay and working conditions] can bargain away a significant fraction of potential profits."[6]

The final factor in Porter's framework is industry rivalry; as he notes, "some forms of competition, notably price competition, are highly unstable and quite likely to leave the entire industry worse off from the standpoint of profitability."[7] One measure of rivalry is in advertising spending. For example, the advertisements of Apple, the highly successful manufacturer of computers and iPhones, often targeted its rival, Microsoft, the software company that controls a large part of the market for software for personal computers. In the ads, Apple portrayed itself as a young, hip person, whereas Microsoft was a middle-aged "nerd." Another is how much money competitive businesses in a sector are investing in developing new technology.

Rivalry is highest in markets in which sales are not growing or products are undifferentiated—they are very similar to one another. Porter says companies could try to change these conditions. "Focusing selling efforts on the fastest growing segments of the industry ... can reduce the impact of industry rivalry," Porter observes.[8] Finding a way to escape market rivalry allows businesses to be more profitable.

Language and Expression

Porter makes clear in *Competitive Strategy* that he is writing for practitioners (that is, those actively involved in managing businesses or advising the people who are). As such, he sees his work as creating a bridge between scholars who do pure research and people occupied with the cut and thrust of business competition. As such, he was reaching across the chasm between actual business and stylized models from the world of theory.

As well as affecting his language (which is easily understood by anyone, and avoids mathematics or technical terms used in academic economics), his approach affected the work's focus.

For Porter, writing for practitioners and in a language accessible to anyone meant he could examine issues that academic work had neglected. Academic economists, he argues, had been focusing mainly on industries, considering individual companies as equal in highly abstract models. Similarly, managers were absent in academic models.

This approach extends to the questions Porter addresses in *Competitive Strategy*: what the nature of competition in an industry means for company behavior, how to push profits up (a concern for businesses) rather than down (a concern for society, government policy, and for consumers), and how to understand competition among a small number of companies whose behavior affects each other.

1. Michael E. Porter, *Competitive Strategy: Techniques for Analyzing Industries and Competitors*, 2nd ed. (New York: Free Press, 1998), 7.
2. Porter, *Competitive Strategy*, 9.
3. Porter, *Competitive Strategy*, 23.
4. Porter, *Competitive Strategy*, 24.
5. Porter, *Competitive Strategy*, 26.
6. Porter, *Competitive Strategy*, 28.
7. Porter, *Competitive Strategy*, 17.
8. Porter, *Competitive Strategy*, 22.

MODULE 6
SECONDARY IDEAS

KEY POINTS

- After looking at the five forces,* *Competitive Strategy* looks at three approaches that Porter calls generic strategies;* these help businesses decide how to position themselves in their market.

- The three strategies are: offering the lowest prices; offering a differentiated product; focusing strongly on a niche market.

- Porter also provides analyses and strategies for overlooked but potentially profitable niches, including businesses in declining markets and businesses in rapidly globalizing* industries (industries increasingly operating across continental borders).

Other Ideas

The secondary themes of Michael E. Porter's *Competitive Strategy: Techniques for Analyzing Industries and Competitors* are how businesses can pursue a competitive advantage* by aiming at lower cost, a differentiated product, or a narrow focus on a target audience.

Lower cost—which he refers to as cost leadership*—aims at attracting the most price-sensitive customers. They will often have little brand loyalty, and will be easily targeted by competitors who can manage a still lower price.

Differentiation* (making a company's product different from similar products sold by other companies) is aimed at less price-sensitive customers who are not being served well by the existing

130

market. It tends to be done best by larger companies.

Smaller companies are better suited to a niche strategy—identifying a narrower target market, and looking closely at its distinct needs.

These three approaches, which Porter calls "generic strategies," should be used alongside looking to his five forces to see where a company's competitive position is weakest. Alternatively, a company can try to reshape the five forces by differentiation—that is, trying to make its product different from that of its competitors. Or it can invest to erect entry barriers to dissuade new competitors, such as patents on new technologies (legal protections against their being copied), or spending heavily on new facilities. Through this process, called positioning,* a company adapts to the competitive environment around it.

The idea that a business can choose its strategy in this way was introduced by *Competitive Strategy*. Until this point, following the writings of the influential strategist Bruce Henderson* and the broad acceptance of the experience curve,* the general belief had been that there was precisely one strategy for all companies to follow—pursuing more market share.

Porter's important innovation was to point out that profitability, not market share, is the real goal for a business to pursue—and small businesses may also be very profitable. This means there are different approaches a company can employ.

> "Effectively implementing any of these generic strategies usually requires total commitment and supporting organizational arrangements that are diluted if there is more than one primary target."
>
> —— Michael E. Porter, *Competitive Strategy: Techniques for Analyzing Industries and Competitors*

Exploring the Ideas

According to Porter, cost leadership (offering the lowest prices) "requires aggressive construction of efficient-scale facilities, vigorous pursuit of cost reductions from experience, tight cost and overhead control, avoidance of marginal customer accounts, and cost minimization in areas like [research and development], service, sales force, [and] advertising."[1] Having a lower cost relative to competitors, he adds, "becomes the theme running through the entire strategy."[2]

It is helpful for this strategy if a company can have a high relative market share. Achieving this might require start-up losses, says Porter, such as heavy investment in state-of-the-art equipment, or favorable access to raw materials.

The strategy is a particularly appealing one, according to Porter, because it "protects the firm against all five competitive forces."[3] Bargaining with buyers and suppliers will "only continue to erode profits until those of the next efficient competitor are eliminated." In this process the less efficient competitors "will suffer first" in the face of competitive pressures.[4]

A business might attract price-sensitive customers by having the lowest prices, or the lowest ratio of price to value. A company might try to use its assets better than its competitors (an airline could turn around its flights more quickly; a restaurant could more quickly clear tables to allow the next guests to sit down). Costs of equipment or fixed costs, such as rent, staffing, or lighting, are known as sunk (that is, already paid-for) costs. If more product can be squeezed out, then these costs can then be divided over more units of product.

Another approach is for a company to market itself by offering standardized, no-frills products to purchasers, like the Irish low-cost airline Ryanair.* A downside to the strategy includes lower customer loyalty, because price-sensitive customers will switch when a similar—if slightly better—option becomes available.

Porter's second strategy—differentiation—may suit larger companies better. It targets customers who are slightly less price-sensitive, and are underserved by the existing market. It creates "something that is perceived *industry-wide* as being unique."[5] A company choosing this strategy should try to avoid a product that could easily be copied by competitors. It could do this by having unique technical skills, especially trained staff, or patents for new technologies.

Possible approaches to differentiating can take many forms, particularly good design or top-of-the-line brand image (the German luxury car manufacturer Mercedes Benz, for example).[6] Another approach might be excellent customer service or a reliable dealer network. Porter uses the US construction machinery company Caterpillar Inc. as an example, because it is "known not only for its dealer network and excellent spare parts availability but also for its extremely high-quality durable products."[7] However, Porter adds, "It should be stressed that the differentiation strategy does not allow the firm to ignore costs, but rather that they are not the primary strategic target."[8]

Finally, Porter's niche strategy—he also calls this "focus"—could work best for smaller businesses. Smaller groups of target clients might not provide enough volume for larger companies to recoup their investments in fixed costs. A target market might be geographic, it might be demographic (that is, a specific section of a population, such as a particular age bracket or ethnic group), or it might have to do with lifestyles.[9]

This strategy involves looking closely at the needs of a distinct group and its specialized needs. "The entire focus strategy is built around serving a particular target very well," he says.[10] This strategy hopes to generate a high degree of product loyalty. Competitive advantage in this case comes from innovation and brand marketing, not from the same strict attention to efficiency as the cost leadership strategy.

Porter observes that this focus (that is, niche) strategy is linked to the other two. "Even though the focus strategy does not achieve low cost or differentiation from the perspective of the market as a whole, it does achieve one or both of these positions vis-à-vis its narrow market target."[11]

Overlooked

Competitive Strategy is chiefly known for introducing Porter's five competitive forces, and his three generic strategies for responding to these forces.

Porter does, however, provide many other helpful insights into competing in particular types of industries. Chapter 12 of the book, for example, looks at declining industries, like cigar manufacture or bookbinding, while Chapter 13 looks at industries undergoing rapid globalization, like the automotive industry at present. Neither of these two examples is frequently cited by other writers or practitioners—certainly not as often as the five forces and three generic strategies, which are referred to (if not always quite correctly) by business executives and consultants the world over. But both contain powerful observations.

For example, Porter observes that the common wisdom is that owners of businesses in declining industries* (industries experiencing a decline in demand) should stop making any new investments, generate as much cash flow as possible, and eventually divest (sell off the business). However, Porter points out that declining industries vary greatly, and some businesses have even done well with heavy new investment. To devise a successful strategy it is necessary to look at remaining pockets of demand— cigars, for instance, are in decline, but the premium segment (high-end cigars) remains. This market segment is price-insensitive and is open to high levels of new product differentiation. There are also buyers in some declining industries who might have to pay costly switching costs (the price of new equipment or training) to begin using another product, such as another computer system.

With globalization, Porter notes, producing for a global market

can allow faster learning, and permit larger economies of scale*—
the greater the number a product is manufactured in, the cheaper
each unit is to manufacture. If underserved market segments exist
in many countries, a company can try to serve the same niche in
several countries at the same time. The market, for example, for
"fair trade" mobile telephones (equipment built according to strict
ethical and environmental standards) may in any single country
be small, but worldwide may be enough for a company to begin
benefiting from economies of scale.

---

1. Michael E. Porter, *Competitive Strategy: Techniques for Analyzing Industries and Competitors*, 2nd ed. (New York: Free Press, 1998), 35.
2. Porter, *Competitive Strategy*, 35.
3. Porter, *Competitive Strategy*, 36.
4. Porter, *Competitive Strategy*, 36.
5. Porter, *Competitive Strategy*, 37.
6. Porter, *Competitive Strategy*, 37.
7. Porter, *Competitive Strategy*, 37.
8. Porter, *Competitive Strategy*, 37.
9. Porter, *Competitive Strategy*, 37.
10. Porter, *Competitive Strategy*, 38.
11. Porter, *Competitive Strategy*, 38–39.

MODULE 7
ACHIEVEMENT

KEY POINTS

* Porter's contribution is located between the rich detail of a business school case study and the highly abstract models of academic economics; he calls this level a "middle-ground framework."

* Part of the book's strength is derived from its stitching together of the fields of industrial organization economics* (inquiry into the structures of firms and markets) and business policy (strategy);* while both look at business behavior, they do not normally engage with each other.

* Limitations include the fact that, as a middle-level analysis, the book does not take into account contexts that are microeconomic* (inside the firm) or macroeconomic* (in the broader economy); he remedies this in his next book, *Competitive Advantage: Creating and Sustaining Superior Performance*.

Assessing the Argument

To understand competitive forces, Michael E. Porter's *Competitive Strategy: Techniques for Analyzing Industries and Competitors* offers a "middle-ground framework"—a model more generalized than a case study of one company or industry, yet more detailed than an economic model.

As Porter notes, "The essence of formulating competitive strategy is relating the company to its environment."[1] *Competitive Strategy* stresses the idea of strategic choice by a company.

A company achieves this through positioning (a strategic consideration of its products' place in the market) and through profitability.

It is worth noting that Porter's five forces* and three generic strategies* used in the process of positioning (cost, differentiation, focus on a section of the market) follow neither the case-study approach of business schools, nor the modeling approach from economics. Instead they offer what Porter calls "frameworks." As Porter explains, "a framework tries to capture the full richness of a phenomenon with the most limited number of dimensions."[2]

Porter's frameworks occupy a midway point between case studies and models, providing (Porter claims) the smallest number of "core elements that still capture the variation and dimensionality of competition."*[3] A framework's dimensions need to be intuitively grounded, and must make sense to a practitioner (a person running or advising a business). If it fails to do this, a framework will only serve to showcase the education, and justify the invoices, of a professional consultant class.

> *"The chapter on generic strategies was the last chapter to be written. Again, it involved uncomfortable territory. Business school colleagues were saying, 'Too abstract' and 'We can't generalize,' while the economists were saying, 'Where are the statistical tests? What is the model?' It was a very uncomfortable leap."*
>
> ——Nicholas Argyres and Anita McGahan, "An Interview with Michael Porter," *The Academy of Management Executive*

Achievement in Context

The early 1980s, when Porter published *Competitive Strategy*, was a critical juncture in the field of business strategy. The young field was rich in interesting questions, but poor in frameworks to analyze them.[4]

The field had seen promising work in the 1960s and early 1970s. But then in the later 1970s it was neglected when promised successes did not materialize. The big success at the time of Japanese companies, especially automakers, "did not seem to depend on planning as much as it did on quality, corporate and national culture, and management itself,"[5] in the words of one commentator. *Competitive Strategy* launched a second wave in the field of business strategy.

Porter focused on strategy and competition in order to take the discipline in a new direction. However, he also adopts some elements of the work of those who came before him. For example, from the scholar Kenneth Andrews* he takes the usefulness of the concept of strategy, and the important role of senior managers in identifying competitive threats and opportunities in their industry.

From the strategy scholars Paul Lawrence* and Jay Lorsch* he adopts the view that there is no single best way for a business to organize. He builds strongly on the work of the marketing analyst Sidney Schoeffler* in the Profit Impact of Marketing Strategy (PIMS)* by offering an explanation for the hole in the middle* that survey data revealed—the decisive finding that both high-revenue and low-revenue business could be profitable and that profitability was distinct from market share; businesses, Porter argues, should pursue profits.

Since the book came out, Porter's ideas have had great staying power, with business leaders adopting them in a field in which fads are commonplace. It is an indication of just how broadly they have been adopted that, for example, *Fortune* magazine, a leading business publication, called Porter "the most famous and influential business professor who has ever lived."[6]

Part of the book's strength is in stitching together industrial organization and business policy. This was a synthesis that attracted Porter—who after studying business policy at the Harvard Business School went on to study industrial organization under the economics professor Richard Caves* as a doctoral student in business economics. "There were lots of common issues but no real connection between the two fields," Porter said later in an interview.[7]

Limitations

The success of Porter's framework is limited by four factors. The first is that his analysis is focused on what might be called a "meso" level (that is, a level halfway between the macroeconomic and microeconomic), but does not take account of either. In his later books Porter extends his approach and later partly overcomes this limitation with his discussions of the value chain* and clustering* (the concentration of businesses, suppliers,* and personnel in a particular place).

A second limitation is that he does not inquire much into the nature of a company. The five forces might tell a firm that the forces of competition are relaxed enough to compete, but they do not say anything about whether the company is well suited to compete in that market.

A third limitation is that by seeking a middle ground between academic economics and business, Porter loses a certain precision in his concepts. He says, for example, "A firm differentiates itself from its competitors when it provides something unique that is valuable to buyers beyond simply offering a low price."[8] Which is differentiated here, the business or its product?

Finally, Porter's models lend a scientific justification to situations of monopoly* (only one seller of a product or service) or oligopoly* (only a few sellers). Porter's models treat these situations as perfectly normal: the result of businesses positioning themselves in their own self-interest, and with a correct interpretation of competitive forces. But while achieving a monopoly position may possibly be in the interests of the businesses concerned, it is not clear this is something the rest of society should want, especially since markets rely on competition to be efficient and keep prices down.

---

1. Michael E. Porter, *Competitive Strategy: Techniques for Analyzing Industries and Competitors*, 2nd ed. (New York: Free Press, 1998), 3.
2. Nicholas Argyres and Anita McGahan, "An Interview with Michael Porter," *The Academy of Management Executive* 16: 2 (May 2002): 46.
3. Argyres and McGahan, "An Interview," 46.

4. Argyres and McGahan, "An Interview," 41–42.

5. Robert E. Ankli, "Michael Porter's Competitive Advantage and Business History," *Business and Economic History* 2: 21 (1992), 228–36.

6. Geoff Colvin, "There's No Quit in Michael Porter," *Fortune Magazine*, October 15, 2012, accessed February 9, 2016, http://fortune. com/2012/10/15/theres-no-quit-in-michael-porter/.

7. Argyres and McGahan, "An Interview," 43–52.

8. Porter, *Competitive Strategy*, 120.

MODULE 8
PLACE IN THE AUTHOR'S WORK

KEY POINTS

* Porter's focus throughout his life's work has been developing the ideas he first introduced in *Competitive Strategy* (1980); his book *Competitive Advantage: Creating and Sustaining Superior Performance* (1985) looks at competition* from the standpoint of an industry, and *The Competitive Advantage of Nations* (1990) looks at how countries compete with each another economically.

* His second book, *Competitive Advantage*, introduces the idea of the value chain: * the actions or processes a company carries out that can add value and increase competitive advantage.*

* In the third of these books, Porter introduces the idea of clustering*—in which countries gain advantage in particular industries by having high concentrations of related businesses, like film in Hollywood or finance in the City of London.

Positioning

Competitive Strategy: Techniques for Analyzing Industries and Competitors (1980) is Michael E. Porter's first, most widely read, and most influential work on competition, and it set him on a path of exploring different aspects of competition for the rest of his successful career as a scholar.[1] The book is based on an article that he wrote in the *Harvard Business Review* the year before, "How Competitive Forces Shape Strategy."[2] This article drew an instant audience, and received first place in the 1979 McKinsey Award given for the best *Harvard Business Review* article that year. Its principal focus is on how a business should analyze the environment in its sector to work out what its strategy should be if it is to be successful.

Most of Porter's works after *Competitive Strategy* build on the book's ideas in some way. His body of work is vast, with 19 books and 125 articles, but it is worth highlighting two other major books that were well received.

In 1985, Porter published *Competitive Advantage: Creating and Sustaining Superior Performance* as a companion to *Competitive Strategy*.[3] This book looks at competition at the level of industries, just as *Competitive Strategy* looks at it from the point of view of a firm. If his first book was a text for ambitious young executives, his second was for chief executives—company bosses. And if part of the task of *Competitive Strategy* is determining the keys to getting ahead of the competition, *Competitive Advantage* seeks to provide wisdom about how to stay there.

Competitive Advantage introduced a key idea for which Porter is widely known: the value chain.* This is a rough model for a series of activities or processes, each of which adds value, and for which the customer is prepared to pay. Every action of a company, down to training and providing employee benefits, can be a link in the chain in its own right, and a source of advantage over competitors.

Later, in *The Competitive Advantage of Nations* (1990), Porter would expand this viewpoint to take into account how nations compete economically with one another. Among the concepts he introduces is that of a cluster of businesses in the same industry in the same place, benefiting from the sharing of knowledge. An example is a technology hub, like Silicon Valley. This allows Porter to consider how having business clusters of sufficient size is critical to a country's competitiveness.[4]

His other books tend to apply the insights in these three major works to different cases. He has looked a great deal at introducing competition into health care,[5] for example, and many of his other works have applied his principles to particular countries, such as Japan and Sweden.[6]

> "My initial research was in the industrial organization tradition ... There came a time, though, when I decided that I was going to have to stop pursuing the trajectory I was on and take a big leap ... I decided that I would seek a complete framework, drawing not only on statistical tests but on the larger number of case studies that I had by then assembled, and that was when Competitive Strategy was born."
>
> ——Nicholas Argyres and Anita McGahan, "An Interview with Michael Porter," *The Academy of Management Executive*

Integration

The five-forces analysis* and generic strategies* (from his 1980 *Competitive Strategy*) represent one part of Porter's main contribution to business; the value chain (from 1985) is another key concept for which he is known.

Porter introduces the idea of the value chain in a way that comes right to the point: "Competitive advantage cannot be understood by looking at a firm as a whole. It stems from the many discrete activities a firm performs in designing, producing, marketing, delivering and supporting its product. Each of these activities can contribute to a firm's relative cost position and create a basis for differentiation.*"[7]

This is the value chain—not a string of independent activities (although each can be measured independently). Analyzing the value chain, then, is a tool to break down a firm into a collection of strategically important processes, to understand better the effect of each on cost behavior (the way in which a product's cost changes in response to changes in a company's production activity) and differentiation.* Separate activities like design, production, marketing, and delivery, can each, by performing better than those of competitors, bring a competitive advantage.

Porter's concept of the value chain quickly joined his ideas in *Competitive Strategy* on the pages of business textbooks and in management thought. The concept has since been extended beyond individual firms, to connect value chains into a "value system"* by continuing the analysis to look at the suppliers* who supply a company's suppliers, and the buyers who buy products from a company's buyers.

Significance

Much of the significance of Porter's arguments in *Competitive Strategy* can be viewed by looking at how he explores them further in the third of his most important books, *The Competitive Advantage of Nations* (1990).

In *The Competitive Advantage of Nations*, Porter considers

competitiveness, and the forces behind it, at a national level. These concerns come from his worries over dramatic and enduring declines in how competitive American business is—anxieties that he fleshes out with a good deal of evidence.

In the book, Porter also expresses further his frustrations with the limitations of neoclassical economics*—the dominant approach to economics used to study today's global economy, founded on assumptions such as the rational nature of economic decisions made in order to fulfill specific aims. One example he points to is industry clustering: the technology sector grew rapidly in San Francisco's SiliconValley, for example, and not in a place with lower wage rates or office costs; similarly, finance has clustered in the City of London, and cinema in Hollywood. For Porter, clusters cannot be explained by mainstream economic theory; the oversimplified notions that neoclassical economics uses generate very nice models but largely useless conclusions.

Readers praised Porter's 1990 book as a wise response to simplistic criticisms that if other nations had become more competitive than the United States, they must have had help from their governments—that in some way, they cheated.[8] Instead, the text encouraged the United States to consider ways to become more competitive that were more realistic and honest, and less ideological and xenophobic* (responses, that is, that were more than reactions based on a distrust of foreigners).

Since then, his core argument—that countries compete internationally and country competitiveness can be analyzed and measured—has gained a leading place in the management literature. It has not done so, however, in the economics literature. From the viewpoint of economists, international competitiveness is a characteristic of a business, not of a nation. For Porter, this neglect of what he sees as a key issue of our day only confirms his criticism of academic economics.

1. See Ian Jörgensen, "Michael Porter's Contribution to Strategic Management," *Revista Base (Administração e Contabilidade) de UNISINOS*, 5: 3 (2008), 236–38.
2. Michael E. Porter, "How Competitive Forces Shape Strategy," *Harvard Business Review* 57.2 (1979): 137–45.
3. Michael E. Porter, *Competitive Advantage: Creating and Sustaining Superior Performance* (New York: Free Press), 1985.
4. Michael E. Porter, *The Competitive Advantage of Nations* (New York: Macmillan, 1990; 2nd ed., 1998).
5. Michael E. Porter and Elizabeth O. Teisberg, *Redefining Health Care: Creating Value-Based Competition on Results* (Boston, MA: Harvard Business School Press, 2006).
6. Michael E. Porter et al., *Can Japan Compete?* (Basingstoke, UK: Macmillan Publishing, 2000); and Michael E. Porter et al., *Advantage Sweden* (Stockholm: Norstedts Förlag, 1991).
7. Porter, *The Competitive Advantage*, 33.
8. Mariann Jelinek, "Review of *The Competitive Advantage of Nations*," *Administrative Science Quarterly* 37: 3 (1992): 507–10.

SECTION 3
IMPACT

MODULE 9
THE FIRST RESPONSES

KEY POINTS

- While Porter's *Competitive Strategy* sparked great interest in management and academic literature, it has also been criticized for only providing examples to support and illustrate his ideas, even if other examples to support the counterargument could be found.

- Although Porter has answered most of his critiques in detail, he has changed his position in one area; he now believes a "hybrid" strategy, focusing on low-cost products and niche products for a slice of the market, can be profitable.

- Other readers have attempted to add a sixth force to Porter's five forces* (often the government or technology); lawyers have argued that many of the actions he suggests to make it harder for new companies to enter a market may violate antitrust* legislation (law that seeks to promote free-market competition* by preventing things such as agreements by companies on what prices they will all charge).

Criticism

The key critiques of Michael E. Porter's *Competitive Strategy: Techniques for Analyzing Industries and Competitors* are:

- Its approach to understanding rapidly changing modern business is too static.
- Porter's generic strategies* are substitutes for thought rather than spurs to original thinking.
- The underlying beliefs behind the five forces are incorrect.

- His examples and his use of academic literature are selective and incomplete.
- His approach gives too much importance to the role of career managers and consultants, playing down the intuitive knowledge of lower levels of managers and experts in a business, who may have lengthier or more practical knowledge of making and selling products.

The first criticism is that Porter's model is static and a poor fit for describing a modern, rapidly changing industry.[1] A "war of position," in which producers battle to occupy low cost, high features, or niche positions in a market, like that prescribed by Porter's generic strategies, fits an age of "durable products," stable consumer needs, and well-defined markets and competitors. However, in a modern business world "the essence of strategy is not the structure of a company's product and market but the dynamics of its behavior," according to a representative group of critics. Everything is in motion, in this view, and there is no stable structure.[2]

Others have said that the five forces and three strategies are substitutes for thought, not an invitation to ponder key questions. In the words of one critic, "with the advent of generic strategies the task of the executive suddenly became much simpler. Rather than by slogging through a structured analytical process, success could be achieved by following the checklist in the latest airport [best-seller bookshop] book."[3]

The third criticism is that the intellectual beliefs underlying the five forces might be incorrect.[4] One of these assumptions is that buyers, competitors, and suppliers are unrelated, and do not coordinate their approaches, or interact. In a small industry, however, they may very well be in close and constant touch, or in larger ones they may interact at trade fairs and through industrial associations. Rather than only competing, they may see themselves as allies in supporting an industry, its well-being, and its image. Or companies may see would-be competitors as useful sources of help or expertise if their personal relationships are close, or they may outsource to each other when demand for their products is especially high.

Other beliefs that critics have questioned include the assumption that businesses have enough knowledge of the future to accurately do the type of strategic planning outlined in Porter's book. Similarly, critics have questioned the assumption that a company's economic value is augmented by barriers keeping new companies from entering a market, rather than by resources or technical skill; this "occludes [hides] the true role that employees play in the creation of innovation and value," says one group of critics.[5]

Birger Wernerfelt* of the Massachusetts Institute of Technology claims that it is not possible to evaluate an industry's attractiveness—the aim of the five forces—without looking at the resources a business brings to it. Wernerfelt developed a resource-based view* that focuses on the firm and the resources at its disposal rather than on the industry. It uses that bundle of resources as the starting point for measuring competitive advantage.*[6] Although Porter's is more broadly used, this is a major competing theory.

On the issue of the barriers that make it hard for new firms to enter a market, the business scholars Vance Fried* and Benjamin Oviatt* warn about Porter's "general disregard of US antitrust law." This collection of laws seeks to protect competition, by making it illegal for companies to engage in such activities as agreeing on the prices they will each charge. Fried and Oviatt claim that some measures Porter suggests would go against the laws. They add that "risks of violating these laws are inherent in a large number of the defensive and complementary product strategies discussed by Porter, but he generally ignores them."[7] Specifically, the authors say many actions Porter recommends to make it difficult for potential competitors to enter the market may run the risk of violating the Sherman Act,* a major piece of US antitrust legislation passed in 1890.[8]

The fourth criticism is that Porter is selective either with his examples or with his use of the academic literature. William Gartner,* a professor of business studies, suggests Porter did not choose his examples fairly, but rather to support and illustrate his ideas. According to Gartner, "A suspicion is that other examples might be found to make the counterargument and this could lead to some excellent studies."[9]

Part of this criticism, too, is that Porter has a somewhat selective view of the strategic management literature, especially research produced at places other than the Harvard Business School. According to Gartner, "Porter presents some rather weak scenario building strategies, yet he had only to look across the Charles River to see that Massachusetts Institute of Technology has been studying scenario building (system dynamics) for the last twenty years."[10] Scenario building is an approach to strategy that looks at several possible alternative futures—or scenarios—and invites a planner to consider, for example, three different futures: optimistic, pessimistic, and likely.

Finally, the Canadian academic Henry Mintzberg* has offered another approach, which stresses emergent strategy*—a strategy that emerges informally, as an alternative or supplement to senior management's official strategy. This is a response to criticisms that Porter's approach relies too heavily on top management to make all the decisions. According to one critic, "given the highly specialized character and the high-level position accorded to expert strategists," Porter's framework would prevent "any movement towards participatory management"[11] (according to which people employed at different levels in a business's structure can play a role in the business's management).

> "Porter's books overflow with ideas which cry out to be borrowed and put to further use."
> —— William Gartner, "Review of *Competitive Strategy and Competitive Advantage,*" *The Academy of Management Review*

Responses

Porter answers several of these criticisms in the second edition of *Competitive Strategy*.

The first criticism, not being able to analyze and explain

changes in industry, is one of the most frequent attacks against Porter's five forces. Porter addresses this argument by saying "nothing static was ever intended. Each part of the framework—industry analysis, competitor analysis, competitive positioning—stresses conditions that are subject to change."[12]

Other researchers who are sympathetic to Porter have attempted to improve his model by building time into it.[13] One example is to evaluate how consistent the five competitive forces are through past, present, and anticipated time frames, and to detect whether industry structure is fairly constant, or quickly changing.

Porter agrees with Mintzberg about the possibility of emergent strategy existing; for him, "every firm competing in an industry has a competitive strategy, whether explicit or implicit. This strategy may have been developed explicitly through a planning process or it may have evolved implicitly through the activities of the various functional departments of the firm."[14] He argues, however, that emergent (or implicit) strategy will come from each functional department of a company pursuing "approaches dictated by its professional orientation and the incentives of those in charge." For him, this is usually not as good as when top managers set an overall policy for a company. "The sum of these departmental approaches rarely equals the best strategy."[15]

Some critics have stressed that Porter's choice of academic literature and examples is selective, and point to other possible sixth forces such as government policy influencing the market, which might also affect companies' competitive positions. Porter dismisses the suggestion, saying that "there is no [invariable] relationship between the strength and influence of government and the profitability of industry. You can't say that 'government is high, industry profitability is low,' or 'government is low, industry profitability is high.'"[16]

Addressing the criticism that Porter's five forces are somehow incomplete, other sympathetic readers of *Competitive Strategy* have suggested that a sixth force should indeed be added, typically either government or technology. Some of these readers have gone so far as to extend Porter's work in this way; one leading example is the business scholars Adam Brandenburger* and Barry Nalebuff's* work extending *Competitive Strategy*'s arguments by using game theory* (mathematical models of conflict and cooperation used to study the interactions of rational decision-makers).

Brandenburger and Nalebuff look at the relationships between businesses supplying interrelated products, using the results to explain some of the dynamics behind strategic alliances between businesses.[17] They call these goods that complement rather than compete with each other "complementors."* Examples of complementors might be hot dog frankfurters and buns, or gin and tonic.

While Porter has mainly rejected these efforts, he does praise Brandenburger and Nalebuff's extension of his work to consider strategic alliances. He remains convinced that the roles of government or technology must be understood as working through the five forces.[18]

He has, however, revised his thinking about whether hybrid business strategy could exist—whether a business might successfully pursue both a low-cost strategy and a differentiation strategy (producing for a specific slice of the market) at the same time.[19] Some early evidence had suggested that companies pursuing both strategies together might have more success than companies pursuing only one of them.[20]

Conflict and Consensus

Scholars have generally agreed that Porter's text is a masterful synthesis of practical lessons from research in industrial companies over the preceding 20 years. Economists have mostly treated *Competitive Strategy* as a useful source of theories and hypotheses that later, more academic, projects could test. Business and management scholars have taken it as a starting point, with other authors suggesting ways to extend it or make changes to it. As an article in the *Harvard Business Review* put it in 2013, "Michael Porter's five forces model changed the field forever."[21]

Much of this research working to explore Porter's arguments further is presented in journals such as *Strategic Management Journal*, which was formed largely because of new interest in the subject after Porter's *Competitive Strategy*.

As a widely used business text, it certainly comes in for frequent attack. Since 2008, especially, there have been many questions concerning whether or not long-term competitive advantage in fact exists, apart from in markets sheltered from competition by government regulation.[22] Those sharply critical of how corporations were run before the financial crisis of 2008* have seized on this idea that long-term competitive advantage cannot exist as an example of a false promise made by the professional management consultant class.

Alternative approaches continue to be developed, including the resource-based view. Porter's five forces remain more widely read and used, but among a handful of authors, the resource-based view is an attractive competitor.

1. Gregory Dess et al., *Strategic Management* (London: McGraw-Hill, 1995).

2. George Stalk et al., "Competing on Capabilities: The New Rules of Corporate Strategy," *Harvard Business Review* 70.2 (1992): 57–69.

3. Cliff Bowman, "Generic Strategies: A Substitute for Thinking?" *The Ashridge Journal* (Spring, 2008): 1.

4. Kevin Coyne and Somu Subramaniam, "Bringing Discipline to Strategy," *The McKinsey Quarterly* 4 (1996): 14–25.

5. Omar Aktouf et al., "The False Expectations of Michael Porter's Strategic Management Framework," *Problems and Perspectives in Management* 4 (2005): 181–200.

6. Birger Wernerfelt, "A Resource-Based View of the Firm," *Strategic Management Journal* 5.2 (1984): 171–80.

7. Vance Fried and Benjamin Oviatt, "Michael Porter's Missing Chapter: The Risk of Antitrust Violations," *The Academy of Management Executive* 3.1 (1989): 49–56.

8. Fried and Oviatt, "Michael Porter's Missing Chapter," 49.

9. William Gartner, "Review: *Competitive Strategy and Competitive Advantage,*" *The Academy of Management Review* 10.4 (1985): 874.

10. Gartner, "Review," 875.

11. Aktouf et al., "False Expectations," 198.

12. Michael E. Porter, *Competitive Strategy: Techniques for Analyzing Industries and Competitors*, 2nd ed. (New York: Free Press, 1998), xv.

13. Želimir Dulčić et al., "From Five Competitive Forces to Five Collaborative Forces: Revised View on Industry Structure-Firm Interrelationship," *Procedia—Social and Behavioral Sciences* 58 (2012): 1077–84.

14. Porter, *Competitive Strategy*, xxi.

15. Porter, *Competitive Strategy*, xxi.

16. Nicholas Argyres and Anita McGahan, "An Interview with Michael Porter," *The Academy of Management Executive* 16.2 (2002): 46.

17. Adam Brandenburger and Barry Nalebuff, *Co-Opetition* (New York: Crown Business, 1996).

18. Porter, *Competitive Strategy*, xv.

19. Daniel I. Prajogo, "The Relationship Between Competitive Strategies and Product Quality," *Industrial Management & Data Systems* 107.1 (2007): 69–83.

20. Peter Wright et al, "Strategic Profiles, Market Share, and Business Performance," *Industrial Management* (1990): 23–28.

21. Michael Ryall, "The New Dynamics of Competition," *Harvard Business Review* (2013): 80–87.

22. Steve Denning, "What Killed Michael Porter's Monitor Group? The One Force That Really Matters," *Forbes Magazine*, November 20, 2012, accessed January 24, 2016, http://www.forbes.com/sites/stevedenning/2012/11/20/what-killed-michael-porters-monitor-group-the-one-force-that-really-matters/#d4b96f2733c7.

MODULE 10
THE EVOLVING DEBATE

KEY POINTS

* Porter's argument has encouraged the development and widespread application of certain tools to measure his forces, like the four-firm concentration ratio* to measure market share, or the Herfindal-Hirschman index* to measure an individual firm's power in the marketplace.

* After the financial crisis of 2008,* Porter's ideas attracted a great deal of criticism—especially his view that a competitive advantage* could be maintained over time in the absence of government regulation helping one firm or another.

* Although Porter has rejected the criticisms, he does say that if he were writing his book today, he would work in newer research on the power of buyers.

Uses and Problems

The five forces* and three generic strategies*—cost leadership* (keeping the prices of products low), differentiation,* and focus— that Michael E. Porter puts forward in *Competitive Strategy: Techniques for Analyzing Industries and Competitors* have been particularly well received in the field of strategic management. Scholars there have carried out considerable experimental and theoretical analysis of these ideas.[1]

The simplicity of each has helped them be long-lived. Porter's approach was applied by auto manufacturers in the 1980s as it is by Silicon Valley start-ups (young technology companies in California) today. Porter's model led business leaders to think about competition* and profitability, instead of being distracted by less relevant things—as was the focus with older approaches. As a writer in *The Economist* has it: "Few management ideas have been so clear or so intuitively right."[2] The clarity of Porter's approach makes it easily applied in a wide variety of contexts; it grasps the dynamics at the heart of competition.

Porter's framework encourages businesses to pose questions. This, in turn, has led to the widespread use of certain means to measure features of a business. One example is measurement of competitive rivalry, one of the five forces; there are three indexes to do this. One is the four-firm concentration ratio, which measures the market share of the four largest firms; the others are the Herfindal-Hirschman index and the Lerner index,* both of which evaluate the power of an individual firm in the marketplace. Although these three indexes came before *Competitive Strategy* they have become more popular because of the book.

The extent to which Porter's model can still be applied in today's complex business environment—given the Internet and the rapid rate of change and technological advance—has been debated widely. But at the same time, recent data-based research has nonetheless shown a strong link between the five-force analysis and a business's performance. A 2014 statistical study, for example, showed that Porter's model explained performance by the Cooperative Bank of Kenya very well.[3]

> "Except where generated by government regulation, sustainable competitive advantage simply doesn't exist."
>
> —— Steve Denning, "What Killed Michael Porter's Monitor Group? The One Force That Really Matters," *Forbes*

Schools of Thought

With the financial crisis of 2008,* however, Porter's ideas of sustainable competitive advantage were strongly attacked.[4] In this, he was not different from many other management experts, who also attracted criticism from the public and press for their apparent roles in the downturn.

In the political environment following the 2008 financial crisis and the resulting Occupy Movement* that protested about the harm done to society by economic inequality and by the actions of the banks, an establishment figure like Porter was an obvious target.

These criticisms were only strengthened by the 2012 bankruptcy of the Monitor Group,* a business consulting firm that Porter founded together with five Harvard colleagues in 1983, and its sale for a much diminished $116 million. For example, the venture capitalist* Peter Gorski* wrote that "even a blindfolded chimpanzee throwing darts" at the five forces framework could select an equally good business strategy as those proposed by highly paid consultants like Porter[5] ("venture capitalist" here refers to someone who provides initial investment to enable businesses to launch, in the hope of profiting from their eventual success).

In one version of this critique, *Competitive Strategy* was flawed in its aim and the actions it proposed. According to this criticism, its aim was to discover opportunities for long-term excess profits: comfortable low-competition situations, protected by barriers keeping out competitors. Porter held up these opportunities as an easier route for profit-hungry companies. But many economists were concerned that the high profits they might produce imposed unfair costs on the consuming public. According to critics such as the former management consultant Matthew Stewart,* seeking out areas of low competition instead of going to the trouble of designing better products and services, and offering customers and society more value over the long term, presented a lazy route to success.[6]

For these critics, Porter's approach was also flawed because— they argued—long-term competitive advantage does not exist, apart from when it is generated by government regulation (for example, when government grants a monopoly position to a telephone service provider or airline). Also, sustainable above-average profits could not be predicted from the structure of the business sector. Porter's ideas could help to explain success in the past, but were "almost useless in predicting them" in the future, argued Stewart in *The Management Myth: Debunking Modern Business Philosophy* (2009).[7] But not everyone accepted this critique, with the *Wall Street Journal* describing it as "clever but unfair." The newspaper argued that Porter's contributions to understanding businesses' competitive environments are in fact considerably richer than Stewart suggests.[8]

The fact that more than 30 years after its publication Porter is still critiqued for his book *Competitive Strategy* says a great deal about its importance in the business and management world.

In Current Scholarship

Some examples of the broad uses to which *Competitive Strategy*

163

has recently been put include scholarly work in 2015 on the competitive strategies of kindergartens[9] and the Japanese beer market.[10]

Porter has indicated that if he were to rewrite *Competitive Strategy* today, he would adapt the five forces model to build ideas from recent research into his idea of buyer bargaining power.[11] In particular, he says, he would incorporate demand-side economies of scale, such as network* or bandwagon* effects. Network effects describe the effect one user of a good or service has on its value to others—its value depends on the number of other people using it. Telephones are an example (a telephone user has more people to call), as are social networks (with more people to interact with and share pictures with). Bandwagon effects are not very different— the rate of uptake of a product increases the more it is adopted by others. For example, people see their friends using a new technology—perhaps an iPhone at the time of its first appearance in 2007—and they begin thinking about whether to buy one. People's demand for a commodity increases as the number of people using it increases.

1. Peter Wright, "A Refinement of Porter's Strategies," *Strategic Management Journal* 8: 1 (January-February 1987), 93–101.

2. *The Economist* editors, "Competitive Advantage," August 4, 2008, accessed February 9, 2016, http://www.economist.com/node/11869910.

3. Christopher Indiatsy et al., "The Application of Porter's Five Forces Model on Organization Performance: A Case of Cooperative Bank of Kenya Ltd," *European Journal of Business and Management* 6.16 (2014): 75–85.

4. Steve Denning, "What Killed Michael Porter's Monitor Group? The One Force That Really Matters," *Forbes Magazine*, November 20, 2012, accessed January 24, 2016, http://www.forbes.com/sites/ stevedenning/2012/11/20/what-killed-michael-porters-monitor-group-the-one-force-that- really-matters/#d4b96f2733c7.

5. Denning, "What Killed Michael Porter's Monitor Group?".

6. Matthew Stewart, *The Management Myth: Debunking Modern Business Philosophy* (New York: W. W. Norton, 2009), 191.

7. Stewart, *The Management Myth*, 194.

8. Philip Delves Broughton, "Bogus Theories, Bad for Business," *Wall Street Journal*, August 5, 2009, accessed January 24, 2016, http://www.wsj.com/ articles/SB10001424052970204313604574329183 846704634.

9. Yi-Gean Chen, "The Relationship Between Competitive Strategies of Kindergartens with Different Characteristics and Parent Satisfaction," *Journal of Global Business Management* 11.2 (2015): 76–87.

10. Kan Yamamoto, "Kirin: Business Strategies for the Japanese Beer Market," MIT MBA Thesis at the Sloan School of Management, 2015.

11. Nicholas Argyres and Anita McGahan, "Introduction: Michael Porter's 'Competitive Strategy,'" *The Academy of Management Executive* 16.2 (2002): 41–42.

IMPACT AND INFLUENCE TODAY

KEY POINTS

- *Competitive Strategy* remains a key text, and one of the most widely cited, for anyone interested in business strategy and competition.

- Other scholars have come to conclusions similar to those of Porter; that the book has been criticized so much is perhaps due to its popularity.

- For academics, Porter did not provide a single empirically tested idea, offering instead a framework and rich theories for researchers to test afterward; his book has inspired a great deal of further research.

Position

Michael E. Porter's *Competitive Strategy: Techniques for Analyzing Industries and Competitors* has had an immense influence on the business world, particularly in the field of business strategy.* He has so far written 19 books, and more than 125 academic journal articles.[1] He has taught generations of leading executives and consultants at the Harvard Business School, and his ideas on strategy are a vital part of business education worldwide.[2] The Institute on Strategy and Competitiveness, which he heads at Harvard, is dedicated to exploring the ways his research can be applied to the business world.

But it is *Competitive Strategy* for which he is best known. It contains the core of his thought, which he has spent the rest of his career refining and further exploring. *Competitive Strategy* has run to 63 printings, in 19 languages. His second book, *Competitive Advantage: Creating and Sustaining Superior Performance* (1985), has been reprinted at least 38 times.

Competitive Strategy is also a rich source of ideas and theories for exploring how businesses respond to competitive stresses in their environment—situations that make it harder for them to compete. Porter has not only influenced business through his own writing but also indirectly, through the work of other scholars inspired by the ideas he has suggested. According to Google Scholar, an online tool that lists how many times an academic work has been cited, *Competitive Strategy* has been cited nearly 65,000 times.[3]

> "I'll never forget a senior professor telling me that my note on five-forces analysis was 'a good experiment that failed.' "
> ——Nicholas Argyres and Anita McGahan, "An Interview with Michael Porter," *The Academy of Management Executive*

Interaction

Perhaps because the five-force model* is now one of the best known and most broadly used business strategy tools today, critiques have only grown more widespread.

One frequent criticism is that Porter had little good reason for choosing the particular five forces that he did.[4] Another criticism has to do with how well Porter's framework suits modern business environments, which are increasingly complex, changeable, and uncertain. The model seems unable to look ahead in any meaningful way and see how entry barriers, supply chain relationships, or new market entrants all might change—often quickly and without warning.

There have been interesting comments, too, on slightly more theoretical grounds. The Canadian business strategy scholar Henry Mintzberg* makes the case, for example, that low cost is not theoretically different from other types of differentiation, and should just be considered one possible type of differentiation. The type and scope of differentiation, says Mintzberg, should be the two dimensions on which to trace a strategy.[5]

The Continuing Debate

It is worth mentioning, too, the large amount of work based on real-world data that has taken Porter's *Competitive Strategy* as a starting point.

Research that largely confirms Porter's theories can be found in the Korean scholars Linsu Kim* and Yooncheol Lim's* 1998 article "Environment, Generic Strategies, and Performance in a Rapidly Developing Country: A Taxonomic Approach," which looks at companies in South Korea. The authors find *Competitive Strategy*'s generic strategies are more supported by the data than the models of other scholars.[6]

The business scholars Alexander Miller* and Gregory Dess's* 1993 article "Assessing Porter's (1980) Model in Terms of Its Generalizability, Accuracy, and Simplicity" in the *Journal of Management Studies* is typical here, too.[7] It looked at Porter's generic strategies against the outcomes of the Profit Impact of Marketing Strategy (PIMS),* a two-decade-long study that identified variables that accounted for market success. Miller and Dess found that Porter's model, while simple, captured most of the complexity of the issues.

As a broad framework, Porter's view of strategy mainly competes with the resource-based view* of the business as a "bundle of unique resources."[8] Both have their uses. Porter's five forces use an analysis that looks outward, to the surrounding market environment. The resource-based view directs the analysis inward, to what is special about the business and its human, technological, and natural resources. There have also been attempts to create a model that combines the two approaches.[9]

Recently, some have attempted to push Porter's framework further. One fairly typical effort was the "Delta model,"* created at the Massachusetts Institute of Technology (MIT) by the management and strategy scholars Arnoldo Hax* and Dean Wilde.* This was an attempt to look into lasting profitability by focusing on the bond between company and customer. It replaced competition (or even the product itself) as the main issue and instead looked at customers as being in long-term relationships with a company based on transparency and fairness. Research in this direction has focused on developing strategic options that encourage customer bonding—"locking in" customers to the business, and locking them out from competitors.[10] One example is loyalty cards; another could be better computer tools to keep track of frequent customers.

1. Michael Porter, "Curriculum Vitae," accessed February 8, 2016, www.kozminski.edu.pl/uploads/ import/kozminski/pl/default_ opisy_2/3269/1/1/m._porter_-_kandydat_do_tytulu_doktora_honoris__ causa_alk.doc.

2. Geoff Colvin, "There's No Quit in Michael Porter," *Fortune Magazine*, October 15, 2012, accessed January 23, 2016, http://fortune. com/2012/10/15/theres-no-quit-in-michael-porter/ .

3. Google Scholar, "Porter Competitive Strategy," accessed on January 23, 2016, https://scholar.google. com/scholar?q=Porter+Competitive+Strategy&btnG=&hl=en&as_sdt=0%2C9.

4. John O'Shaughnessy, *Competitive Marketing: A Strategic Approach* (Boston, MA: Allen & Unwin, 1984); and Richard J. Speed, "Oh Mr Porter! A Re-Appraisal of Competitive Strategy," *Marketing Intelligence and Planning,* 7: 5/6 (1989): 8–11.

5. Henry Mintzberg, "Generic Strategies: Toward a Comprehensive Framework," in *Advances in Strategic Management* vol. 5, ed. Robert Lamb and Paul Shrivastava (Greenwich, CT: JAI Press, 1988), 1–67.

6. Linsu Kim and Yooncheol Lim, "Environment, Generic Strategies, and Performance in a Rapidly Developing Country: A Taxonomic Approach," *The Academy of Management Journal* 31.4 (1998): 802–27.

7. Alexander Miller and Gregory Dess, "Assessing Porter's (1980) Model in Terms of Its Generalizability, Accuracy, and Simplicity," *Journal of Management Studies* 30 (1993): 553–85.

8. Suzanne Rivard et al., "Resource-Based View and Competitive Strategy: An Integrated Model of the Contribution of Information Technology to Firm Performance," *The Journal of Strategic Information Systems* 15: 1 (2006): 29–50.

9. Yiannis Spanos and Spyros Lioukas, "An Examination into the Causal Logic of Rent Generation: Contrasting Porter's Strategy Framework and the Resource-Based Perspective," *Strategic Management Journal* 22.10 (2001): 907–93.

10. Arnoldo Hax, *The Delta Model: Reinventing Your Business Strategy* (New York: Springer, 2009).

MODULE 12
WHERE NEXT?

KEY POINTS

• The Internet, globalization* (increasing economic, social, and political ties across continental borders) and deregulation* (a move away from government interference in the workings of the market) each have the effect of intensifying competition.* Porter's critics and defenders disagree whether this makes his framework outdated or more relevant.

• Part of the reason Porter's contributions have survived since *Competitive Strategy* first appeared in 1980 is that his forces map neatly on to core areas of microeconomics* (economic action at the level of the individual and community) that do not date easily.

• Porter's ideas are highly influential and extremely widespread. Understanding them correctly—including their limitations and the arguments made by critics against his approach—as well as recognizing when his concepts are being incorrectly applied is crucial in management today.

Potential

Michael E. Porter's *Competitive Strategy: Techniques for Analyzing Industries and Competitors* is helpful for understanding business competition in the fast-changing world and into the near future. His models offer clear ways of thinking through the future effects of today's trends—such as the online world, globalization, and deregulation (ending government regulations that limit things such as which companies can compete in a market).

Today's companies have access to far more information about

their customers, suppliers, and competitors than was available in past years—not least through the Internet.

On the one hand, this might make it easier for a business to research information to make it more competitive, and, for example, to use the five-force analysis.* On the other, it might complicate a company's efforts by intensifying the force of competition—making it easier for customers to find substitute products, lowering the costs to consumers of switching from one company to another, and making prices transparent.

But at the same time, the Internet can help businesses tremendously, by enabling them to set up better and better systems for automated order processing and customer-relationship management and assisting them to differentiate themselves from the competition. And if they are pursuing a niche strategy, the Internet can help companies focus more closely on the desires of a target market.

It may also be worth considering two other important current trends: globalization and deregulation. Globalization extends markets beyond national borders—increasing competition based on price, and eroding the strategy of focusing on a local geographical market (witness the death of the independent corner store). For its part, deregulation—removing government regulation with the aim of increasing competition—makes it easier for new companies to enter a market where regulations may previously have limited competition.

Critics have suggested that the Internet, globalization, and deregulation invalidate Porter's models, or at least require they be drastically revised. In the introduction to the second edition of *Competitive Strategy* Porter replies that these three factors can be understood through his five forces, even without updating the model.[1]

> "The way to transform health care is to realign competition with value for patients. Value in health care is the health outcome per dollar of cost expended. If all system participants have to compete on value, value will improve dramatically."
>
> —— Michael E. Porter, *Redefining Health Care: Creating Value-Based Competition on Results*

Future Directions

One explanation for the durability of *Competitive Strategy*'s five forces is the neatness with which they each map into important areas of microeconomics.

"Supplier's bargaining power" relates to supply and demand theory,* cost and production theory,* and price elasticity,* all of which relate to the relationship between prices and market forces; "customers' bargaining power" relates to the exact same forces as they are influenced by and as they influence customer behavior.*

"Competitive rivalry between current players" relates to market structures,* the number of players or economic actors in the market, the size of the market, and growth rates* (the increase in the market value of the goods and services produced by an economy over time). The threat of substitutes relates to substitution effects* (according to which customers will buy cheaper goods when prices go up); the threat of new entrants to the market relates to market entry barriers*—obstacles to entering a market, such as regulations or patents.

Critics such as the business author Larry Downes,* author of an article titled "Beyond Porter,"[2] take the view that forces like information technology (computers and the Internet), globalization, and deregulation require very different analytic and business tools than those developed at the beginning of the 1980s. Yet defenders of Porter might respond that exaggerating the differences between today's digital economy and what came before is what led to earlier mistakes, like the excesses of the dot-com bubble* that occurred when exaggerated expectations for the earnings of Internet-based companies led investors to drive up their stock prices to very high levels, only to have those prices, and even some whole companies, collapse in the late 1990s.

Another response to Larry Downes's critique is that his argument can be turned against him. He argues that Porter's models are tied too much to the economic conditions of 1980. But the forces he points to as the most important ones today might soon themselves be displaced by other developments—new technologies such as wearable technology and 3D printers, or new forms of regulation coming out of concern for the environment. The bottom-line question, for evaluating Porter's models, is whether they are based in the economic conditions of their time of writing, or whether they capture longer-lasting economic realities that could be applied even in the next digital boom.

Summary

Among books on business and management, *Competitive Strategy* is in a position all its own. All of the top 20 Master of Business Administration (MBA) programs ranked by the *Financial Times* teach Porter's models as part of their strategic management courses.[3] The chief alternative approach is the resource-based theory.* But it is worth noting that Porter's *Competitive Strategy* gathers 2.6 million more hits on Google than its main resource-based view rival, Birger Wernerfelt's* article "A Resource-Based View of the Firm."[4]

Competitive Strategy argues that a business is profitable either by being cheaper, or by being different. There are no alternatives.

Porter's five competitive forces provide an easily usable framework for any business to look at its environment. His three generic strategies likewise offer clear guidance about options from which a company can select in deciding how to compete with rivals in its market.

While critics have raised important points such as the importance of not simply applying a cookie-cutter approach to strategy, Porter's ideas remain the leading wisdom in business strategic management 25 years after the publication of *Competitive Strategy*.

It is important to understand and be able to apply the powerful tools and ideas Michael E. Porter outlines in *Competitive Strategy*. But it is equally important to understand their limitations and the criticisms leveled against them and to be able to recognize when they are being used incorrectly—especially for new students of strategy.

---

1. Michael E. Porter, *Competitive Strategy: Techniques for Analyzing Industries and Competitors*, 2nd ed. (New York: Free Press, 1998), xv.
2. Larry Downes, "Beyond Porter," *Context Magazine*, December 1997.
3. Amir Sasson, "Confining the Five Forces," *BI Strategy Magazine*, November 19, 2013, accessed January 24, 2016, http://www.bi.edu/bizreview/articles/confining-the-five-forces-/.
4. Birger Wernerfelt, "A Resource-Based View of the Firm," *Strategic Management Journal* 5.2 (1984): 171–80.

 **GLOSSARY OF TERMS**

1. **Antitrust law:** law that seeks to promote free-market competition by stopping anti-competitive conduct such as agreements by companies on what prices they will all charge. Notable antitrust laws are the 1890 Sherman Act of the United States, supplemented by the Clayton Act in 1914, and the European Coal and Steel Community agreement of 1951.

2. **Bandwagon effect:** a pattern in which a product grows more popular as more people buy it; the probability an individual will purchase the product increases according to the number of other consumers who have already purchased it.

3. **Boston Consulting Group:** a leading management consulting firm, founded in 1963 in Boston. In 1968 it created the growth-share matrix; its founder, Bruce Henderson, was a great proponent of the experience curve and its implications for strategy.

4. **Cluster Mapping Project:** an effort led by Porter at the Harvard Business School, which began in 2014 and seeks to gather data on the presence of clusters in regional economies within the United States. Mapping clusters—regional concentrations of related businesses—is meant to assist regions and businesses in better understanding their competitive position.

5. **Clusters:** a concentration of businesses, suppliers, and personnel in a particular place. Michael Porter popularized the term in his 1990 book *The Competitive Advantage of Nations*. Silicon Valley is an example in technology, as is the City of London in finance or the French winemaking areas of Burgundy or Bordeaux in wine.

6. **Comparative advantage:** a theory first developed by the British economist David Ricardo in 1817, according to which nations and other agents will specialize in producing the good in which they are most efficient (the good they can make at the lowest marginal cost), and engage in international trade to purchase all other goods.

7. **Competition:** a rivalry among sellers to increase their profits, market share, and volume of sales. Classical economists such as the British economist Adam Smith in his 1776 *The Wealth of Nations* described competition as providing an incentive for firms to innovate and become more efficient.

8. **Competitive advantage:** qualities that permit an organization to outperform competitors. These may permit it (Michael E. Porter claims) to offer a lower cost

than its rivals, or to provide a differentiated product that its competitors are not supplying, but for which there is a market.

9. **Competitive strategy:** the means available to business owners seeking to increase the profitability of their business over others.

10. **Complementors:** in many extensions of Porter's five forces model, these are businesses that sell products or services that complement those sold by another business—makers of printers and paper, for example, or distillers of gin and bottlers of tonic. The concept was first introduced by the business scholar Adam Brandenburger.

11. **Conglomerate strategy:** a business adding new goods or services to diversify into a different market unrelated to its current business.

12. **Contingency theory:** the approach that there is not one best method of leadership, but that ideal leadership differs based on the task and environment. The approach could be contrasted with Weber's work on bureaucracy or Taylor's on scientific management, both of which presented a single ideal form of management.

13. **Corporate social responsibility:** a concept that first became popular in the 1960s, holding that corporations have an obligation both to contribute to the communities and environments in which they operate and to create value for shareholders. This might include support for charity, buying fairly traded materials, and contributing to waste and pollution reduction.

14. **Cost and production theory:** relates to the creation of economic well-being through a production process, using resources to create a suitable good or service, with a particular form, quantity, and distribution.

15. **Cost leadership:** the pursuit of a competitive advantage by having the lowest operating costs in the industry, through a combination of efficiency, scale, experience, technology, and standardized products, being able therefore to offer customers the lowest price.

16. **Customer behavior:** the study of buyers and their decision-making processes, including how friends and other reference groups influence them. It breaks down the buying process into recognition of a problem, searching for information, a choice to purchase a product, and its actual purchase.

17. **Declining industries:** industries that experience negative growth or are stagnant

because of declining demand for their products—industries in which unit sales are in absolute decline over a sustained period.

18. **Delta model:** an approach to strategic management based on a business's relationship with its customers, rather than on competition—as in the case of Porter's five forces. Its key points include locking in customers as a source of sustainable profitability. It was developed by the management and strategy scholars Dean Wilde and Arnoldo Hax.

19. **Deregulation:** the reduction of government rules, restrictions, or oversight in any sectors of the economy. Deregulation was a heavy feature of the economic programs of President Reagan in the United States and Prime Minister Thatcher in the United Kingdom.

20. **Differentiation:** making a product different from similar products. The idea is proposed in 1933 by Edward Chamberlin in his *Theory of Monopolistic Competition*. It is also one of Michael E. Porter's generic strategies.

21. **Dot-com bubble:** a speculative bubble that began in 1997 and peaked in March 2000, which saw stock market values increase quickly from growth in the Internet sector. The bubble collapsed from 1999 to 2001, with some companies, such as pets.com, failing completely, and others, such as eBay and Amazon, experiencing drastic losses in value, before going on to surpass their bubble-era peaks.

22. **Economic geography:** the study of the location of economic activities. It includes such research as spatial modeling to explain how industrial clusters emerge. The role of knowledge, transport costs, and positive externalities are all-important concepts in most research, explaining why industries sometimes develop faster in some areas than others.

23. **Economies of scale:** setup under which cost advantages come to businesses with increasing output, as fixed costs (like the costs of machinery or buildings) are spread over more units of output, making per-unit costs decrease as scale grows.

24. **Emergent strategy:** the view that strategy develops naturally over time as a company gains knowledge about which sets of behaviors work in practice.

25. **Experience curve:** an observation that the more a task has been performed, the less time is required to perform it again. From 1968 on, Bruce Henderson and the

Boston Consulting Group promoted its implications for strategy.

26. **Financial Crisis of 2008:** a severe global economic downturn that saw a worldwide drop in stock markets, many banks needing to be rescued by governments, and unemployment and drops in housing markets in many parts of the world. It was the beginning of a global decline that lasted until 2012.

27. **Five forces** and **five-force analysis:** a framework proposed by Michael E. Porter to understand market competition better. The forces include the threat of new entrants and substitute products, the number of rival businesses, and the bargaining powers of buyers and suppliers. According to the approach, it is easier to turn a profit in less fiercely competitive industries.

28. **Fortune 500:** an annual list compiled by *Fortune* magazine featuring 500 of the largest US corporations in terms of revenue. It was first published in 1955.

29. **Four-firm concentration ratio:** a measure of how much an industry is controlled by a small number of firms—that is, how much a given industry is an oligopoly. It measures the total market share of the four largest firms in the industry.

30. **Game theory:** mathematical models of conflict and cooperation used to understand the behavior of rational decision-makers. It was developed in the 1940s by mathematicians, and now is being used as a leading research method in economics and across the social sciences.

31. **General Electric:** an American multinational company, founded in 1892 by the inventor Thomas Edison, that normally features among the 10 largest US firms by revenue on the Fortune 500 list. Half its revenue is derived from financial services; it also has substantial presences in the energy and consumer appliance sectors.

32. **Generic strategies:** three options for businesses, proposed by Porter, concerned with the pursuit of competitive advantage in their chosen market. Businesses can either choose to compete on the grounds of lowest cost, they can differentiate themselves from other products, or they can focus on a target niche market segment.

33. **Globalization:** the process of integration of nations, accelerated by advances in transportation and communications. Ideas, technologies, and goods are all increasingly exchanged. It began on a large scale with the Industrial Revolution in the nineteenth century, and has been accelerating since then.

34. **Great Depression:** a decrease in living standards and employment, which began in 1929 in the United States, spread around the world, and lasted until the late 1930s. Worldwide gross domestic product (GDP) fell by 15 per cent from 1929 to 1932. Unemployment in the United States rose to 25 per cent.

35. **Growth rates:** the increase in the market value, adjusted for inflation, of the goods and services produced by an economy over time. Normally the rates are measured as the percentage increase of real gross domestic product, or GDP.

36. **Growth-share matrix:** a chart created by Bruce Henderson's Boston Consulting Group in 1970 to assist businesses analyzing their product lines. It plots a business's units or products by their market shares and growth rates, dividing them as cash cows, dogs, question marks, and stars.

37. **Herfindal-Hirschman index:** a measure of a business's market share within an industry, and the amount of competition within the sector.

38. **Hole in the middle problem:** a criticism raised by Porter of the idea that companies always should seek higher market share. He found that both low-revenue and high-revenue firms could be highly profitable, and it is profitability rather than market share that a company should seek. Firms in the middle were the least profitable.

39. **Industrial organization economics:** a field of study within economics that looks at the structure of firms and markets considering complications that prevent perfect competition, such as transaction costs, limited information, and barriers to entry of new firms.

40. **Industry structure:** the number of companies competing for the same business, the numbers of customers and suppliers, new entrants, and the threat of substitute products. The insight behind the concept of industry structure is that a firm's profitability depends on the market environment in which it is operating, and not only its own behavior.

41. **Lerner index:** a measure of a firm's market power, devised in 1934 by the Russian-born British economist Abba Lerner. It reflects the ability of a firm to raise the market price of a good or service over marginal cost.

42. **Macroeconomics:** the branch of economics dealing with national, regional, and global economies, and indicators including gross domestic product,

unemployment rates, and inflation.

43. **Managerial revolution:** a concept associated with the work of the management scholar James Burnham, author of *The Managerial Revolution* (1941). Burnham argued that managers had become a new modern ruling class, and that unrestricted capitalism was being replaced by a more planned and centralized society and economy.

44. **Marginal cost:** the extra cost of producing one more unit. Firms decide how much of a good to produce based on comparing the marginal cost with the sale price. If it is less than the sale price, the company will continue to produce until the two are equal.

45. **Market entry barriers:** obstacles that make it difficult for a business to enter a market. These might be regulations, intellectual property such as patents, licensing and education requirements, and economies of scale enjoyed by the leading businesses already in the sector.

46. **Market entry:** the process of a business entering a new market. It might do this by setting up an entity in the new market, by exporting directly, using a reseller or distributor, or producing products in the target market.

47. **Market segmentation:** a marketing strategy that involves dividing a large market into smaller groups of customers with common needs.

48. **Market share:** in units or revenue, the percentage of a market accounted for by a particular business. Market share is an indicator of market competitiveness—how well a business is doing against its competitors.

49. **Market size:** the number of people (or companies) in a market who are potential buyers or sellers of a product or service.

50. **Market structure:** a measure of the number of firms producing a product. In a monopoly, there is one; in an oligopoly, there are several.

51. **Marketing myopia:** a term used to describe the mistake made by businesses that focus mainly on selling products rather than on meeting the needs of customers. It is the title of a 1960 article by Theodore Levitt published in the *Harvard Business Review*.

52. **Mass production:** the production of large numbers of standardized goods, especially if done with the use of an assembly line. It became widespread with the Industrial Revolution in the late nineteenth century, and especially after Henry Ford pioneered the mass production of the Model T Ford car in 1908.

53. **Microeconomics:** a branch of economics that looks at individuals and firms and their decision-making.

54. **Monitor Group:** a business strategy consulting group founded by Michael E. Porter and five colleagues associated with the Harvard Business School in 1983. The firm was heavily hit by the 2008 economic crisis, and filed for bankruptcy at the end of 2012. Deloitte acquired it in January 2013.

55. **Monopoly:** a market in which one supplier (in many cases a company) controls the supply of a good or service that does not have a close substitute, and can set its price considerably above the marginal cost of production.

56. **Monopsony:** a market in which one buyer confronts multiple sellers of a product. The buyer therefore has a great deal of power to set the price.

57. **Neoclassical economics:** a set of twentieth-century approaches to economics that focuses on concepts such as marginal returns, maximized utility, equilibrium, and others. Neoclassical economics is the dominant form of economics used to study today's global economy.

58. **Network effect:** the effect one user of a good or service has on its value to other people. An example is having a telephone or being on a social network—it is more useful for me to buy a telephone or be on a social networking site if you do likewise.

59. **Occupy Movement:** a series of linked protests staged in many cities around the world against what were seen as injustices in the global financial system. It began in New York in September 2011 as the Occupy Wall Street Movement.

60. **Oligopoly:** a market in which there is a small number of businesses selling a product. With a small number of businesses in a market, they may collude to keep prices up or reduce risks; or, alternatively, they may compete more fiercely.

61. **Opportunity cost:** the value of the best alternative action to one that is taken—waiting, for example, for a customer service representative costs money corresponding to the amount of time you are waiting, and the wage rate of your

time. That opportunity cost represents the money you might have earned had you not been so engaged.

62. **Organization of Petroleum Exporting Countries (OPEC):** intergovernmental organization with 13 members consisting of nations that export petroleum, including Iran, Iraq, Kuwait, Libya, the United Arab Emirates, and Saudi Arabia. OPEC was established in September 1960.

63. **PEST analysis:** a framework for noting political, economic, social, and technological factors in a business's environment. It sometimes is expanded to SLEPT if including legal factors, or changed to PESTLE to include legal and environmental factors.

64. **Porter hypothesis:** a suggestion, made by Michael E. Porter in an article in 1995, that stricter environmental regulation might bring about efficiency and innovation in a market, which would in turn make a market more competitive.

65. **Position/positioning:** the niche that a brand occupies relative to its competitors. It is largely achieved through advertising—marking the product or service as budget or premium, entry-level or high-end, or promoting the distinctive features of the brand, such as what it can do that competitors' products cannot.

66. **Price elasticity:** a measure of how much the demand for a good or service changes in response to a change in its price.

67. **Production orientation:** when a company focuses on the good or service it produces; normally this is contrasted with a (superior) market orientation, which involves a focus on the desires of the customer.

68. **Profit Impact of Marketing Strategy (PIMS):** a survey, begun in the 1960s by Sidney Schoeffler and lasting until 1983, which researched 2,600 business units within 200 companies, and identified 37 variables that accounted for most business success. These included a strong market position, a high quality product, lower costs, and market growth.

69. **Resource-based view:** a way of conceiving of a business's competitive advantage by looking primarily at the resources—tangible or intangible—at the disposal of the business. To enjoy a lasting competitive advantage, a business's resources must be valuable, rare, hard to copy, and nonsubstitutable.

70. **Ryanair:** an Irish low-cost airline founded in 1984 and presently managed by chief executive Michael O'Leary. It is the busiest airline internationally by the number of passengers. It pioneered a low-cost business model in the context of deregulation of European aviation in 1997 and pioneered online ticket booking and no-frills, low-cost travel.

71. **Sherman Act:** an 1890 antitrust law permitting the US federal government to go after trusts and monopolies in order to promote competition in the economy.

72. **Stanford Research International:** a research institute founded in 1946 by Stanford University in California to support economic development in the surrounding region.

73. **Strategic fit:** a measure of how well the structure and capabilities of a firm matches its external environment. It is related to the resource-based view, which links profitability and lasting competitive advantage with a company's resources and capabilities.

74. **Strategic positioning:** a company's decisions about how it will create value differently from its rivals; typically, these involve a decision about whether to charge a premium price or seek lower costs for the company.

75. **Strategy:** a plan to achieve goals in a situation of uncertainty. Strategy emerged as a topic in business and management in the 1960s; previously it was associated chiefly with diplomatic or military and naval matters.

76. **Structure-conduct-performance paradigm:** a model in industrial organization economics, developed by the economist Joe Bain, which looks at how market structure affects a business's performance.

77. **Substitutes:** alternative, cheaper products or services.

78. **Substitution effects:** the effects caused by changes in the price of an item— when the price goes up, customers will buy more lower-priced goods and fewer more expensive ones. They will substitute less expensive goods for ones whose price has increased.

79. **Suppliers:** companies that supply resources a business requires to function—a wheat farm for a flour maker, a flour mill for a baker.

80. **Supply and demand theory:** an economic model of determining price in a market

under conditions of competition. In a market, the price for a good will settle at the point at which the quantity supplied will match the quantity demanded.

81. **Sustainable competitive advantage:** a long-term advantage that cannot easily be duplicated or improved upon by rivals. This may consist of superior access to natural or human resources or barriers to entry in the market that shield a company from competition.

82. **Switching costs:** costs that a customer or business incurs when it changes suppliers, products, or brands.

83. **SWOT analysis:** a technique to analyze a business's Strengths, Weaknesses, Opportunities, and Threats. It was popularized by the Stanford Research Institute and Albert Humphrey in the 1960s and 1970s.

84. **Value chain:** a set of discrete activities a business performs to produce a product or service. The idea is to think of a firm's activities as a series of processes—the outputs of some processes being inputs into later ones. Michael E. Porter proposes the concept in his 1985 work *Competitive Advantage*.

85. **Value system:** The idea of a value system extends the concept of a value chain beyond individual firms—linking processes between the companies that produce a company's supplies and buy a company's products.

86. **Venture capitalist:** an investor who specializes in providing capital to companies in their early stages.

87. **Vertical integration:** a setup in which each element in the supply chain for a good or service is owned by a single company. The US industrialist Andrew Carnegie provided an early example in his steel manufacture.

88. **World War II:** a global war that lasted from 1939 to 1945, directly involving more than 100 million people from 30 countries and with $50 - 85$ million deaths. Its results included decolonization in Asia and Africa, the Cold War between rival blocs led by the United States and the Soviet Union, and political integration within Europe.

89. **Wright-Patterson Air Force Base:** one of the US Air Force's largest bases, situated near Dayton, Ohio. Test flights of newly developed aircraft are frequently carried out there.

90. **Xenophobia:** an aggressive dislike or fear of people from other countries or cultures.

PEOPLE MENTIONED IN THE TEXT

1. **Alexander the Great** or **Alexander III of Macedon (365–323 B.C.E.)** was king of the Southern European nation of Macedonia from 336, of Persia (from 330), and pharaoh of Egypt (from 332). He was founder of a number of cities that bear his name, such as Alexandria in Egypt, and responsible for the widespread diffusion of Hellenic (ancient Greek) culture. His tutor was the philosopher Aristotle.

2. **Kenneth Andrews (1916–2005)** was a lecturer at the Harvard Business School and an important early figure in the spread of the concept of business strategy, together with his colleague Alfred Chandler. For Andrews, managers obtain authority by treating subordinates with respect, and organizations, to survive, require effectiveness (the ability to accomplish shared goals) and efficiency (satisfying the motives of individuals).

3. **Joseph ("Joe") Bain (1912–91)** was an economist at the University of California, Berkeley, where he was an important figure in industrial organization economics. He developed the concept of barriers to entry to explain industry performance, and worked on questions relating to industry concentration as well.

4. **Chester Barnard (1886–1961)** was a business academic known for his 1938 book *The Functions of the Executive.*

5. **Adam Brandenburger** was an academic at the Harvard Business School from 1987 to 2002, and coauthor (with Barry Nalebuff) of *Co-Opetition* (1996), which looks at situations in which companies may choose to cooperate rather than compete.

6. **Richard Caves (b. 1931)** is an economics professor at Harvard, who works especially in the area of industrial organization.

7. **Alfred DuPont Chandler (1918–2007)** was a business historian at Harvard Business School who received the Pulitzer prize for history for his 1977 book, *The Visible Hand: The Managerial Revolution in American Business.* In this book and elsewhere, he was significant in introducing and popularizing the concept of business strategy.

8. **Gregory Dess** is a management academic in Texas, known mainly for an article

in the *Academy of Management Review* that looks at connections between a firm's entrepreneurial behavior and high performance.

9. **Larry Downes** is an author and business academic in the United States, known especially for his book, coauthored with Chunka Mui, *Unleashing the Killer App: Digital Strategies for Market Dominance* (2008).

10. **Henry Ford (1863–1947)** was an American industrialist and car manufacturer known especially for pioneering the assembly line and mass marketing the automobile to the middle classes.

11. **Vance Fried** is the Riata Professor of Entrepreneurship at Oklahoma State University.

12. **William Gartner (b. 1953)** is an American business studies professor at the California Lutheran University in Thousands Oaks, California, and the Copenhagen Business School in Denmark. He is an expert in entrepreneurship.

13. **Peter Gorski** is a venture capitalist and project manager in the United States, as well as an occasional author.

14. **Arnoldo Hax** is the Alfred P. Sloan Professor of Management Emeritus at the Massachusetts Institute of Technology (MIT), and specializes in strategic management. He is known for coauthoring the book *The Delta Project: Discovering New Sources of Profitability in a Networked Economy* with Dean Wilde in 2001.

15. **Bruce Henderson (1915–92)** was founder in 1963 of the Boston Consulting Group (BCG), and continued as its president and chief executive until 1980. He was very influential in the firm, deciding that its emphasis would lie in strategy consultancy. During his time at BCG, he played a major role in diffusing the concepts of the experience curve and growth-share matrix.

16. **Albert Humphrey (1926–2005)** was a management consultant and business academic who, during his time at the Stanford Research Institute, was influential in spreading the SWOT analysis.

17. **Linsu Kim** is professor of management at Korea University in South Korea.

18. **Mark Kramer** is a frequent collaborator with Michael E. Porter in the *Harvard*

Business Review, and is especially known for his work on the concept of shared value.

19. **Paul Lawrence (1922–2011)** was the professor of organizational behavior at the Harvard Business School, known especially for his work with the organizational theorist Jay Lorsch on differentiation and integration in complex organizations.

20. **Theodore Levitt (1925–2006)** was a German-born economist at the Harvard Business School especially known for the 1960 article "Marketing Myopia" in the *Harvard Business Review*, and for publicizing the concept of globalization.

21. **Yooncheol Lim** is an academic at the Korea Advanced Institute of Science and Technology in South Korea.

22. **Jay Lorsch (b. 1932)** is an organizational theorist at the Harvard Business School, especially known for his contributions to contingency theory—which argues that there is not a single superior style of leadership, but that leadership must take into account the environment, and aim at such goals as winning the respect of followers, providing adequately structured tasks, and having the required formal authority.

23. **Joan Magretta** is a senior associate at the Institute for Strategy and Competitiveness at the Harvard Business School, which Porter runs. Previously she has been the strategy editor of the *Harvard Business Review*, and a consultant at Bain & Company. She wrote a 2011 book on Porter, called *Understanding Michael Porter: The Essential Guide to Competition and Strategy*.

24. **Roger Martin** is dean of the University of Toronto's Rotman School of Business.

25. **Alexander Miller** is a business academic at the University of Tennessee. Among his publications is a textbook published in 1997 called *Strategic Management*.

26. **Henry Mintzberg (b. 1939)** is a Canadian academic and the Cleghorn Professor of Management Studies at McGill University, where he has taught since 1968. A specialist in business strategy, he takes a critical attitude toward received wisdom and prolific practice in management and management consultancy. He has stressed the importance of what he calls emergent strategy, arising informally

within an organization—as opposed to deliberate strategy imposed by senior management, often with the assistance of consultants.

27. **Barry Nalebuff** is a researcher working on business strategy and game theory, and is the Milton Steinbach Professor of Management at the Yale School of Management. One book for which he is especially known is *Co-Opetition* (1996), coauthored with Adam Brandenburger, which looks at situations in which companies may cooperate with one another.

28. **Benjamin Oviatt** is an associate professor in the school of management at Georgia State University.

29. **Philip II of Macedon (382–336 B.C.E.)** was king of the ancient Greek kingdom of Macedon from 359 until his assassination, greatly expanding Macedonian territory in that time. He was father of Alexander the Great.

30. **David Ricardo (1772–1823)** was a British economist. He is best remembered for his work on comparative advantage, claiming that a nation should concentrate on those industries in which it is most competitive internationally. He served as a reformist member of parliament for the last four years of his life.

31. **Sidney Schoeffler** is a marketing analyst; he was one of the founders of the Profit Impact of Marketing Strategy research project, begun at General Electric in the 1960s, which looked into why some business units were more profitable than others, and evaluated them in terms of their market position and strategies.

32. **Herbert Simon (1916–2001)** was an American academic and student of decision-making who received the Nobel Prize in Economics in 1978. One of his contributions was to discuss decision-making in the context of uncertainty.

33. **Matthew Stewart (b. 1963)** is an author and philosopher living in Boston, who worked as a management consultant after completing a DPhil in philosophy at the University of Oxford in 1988. He wrote critically about his experiences as a management consultant, and about the consultancy industry, in his book *The Management Myth: Debunking the Modern Philosophy of Business*, published in 2009 by W. W. Norton.

34. **Frederick Winslow Taylor (1856–1915)** was one of the first management

consultants and an American mechanical engineer. In a 1911 book, *The Principles of Scientific Management*, he sought to apply principles from engineering to making industries more efficient. He was one of the leaders of the Efficiency Movement, which also is called Taylorism.

35. **Mark Twain (1835–1910)** is the pen name of the American author Samuel Clemens, author of *The Adventures of Tom Sawyer* in 1876 and its sequel *Adventures of Huckleberry Finn* in 1885. He was the subject of a doctoral dissertation by Kenneth Andrews, subsequently a leading management scholar.

36. **Birger Wernerfelt (b. 1951)** is a Danish economist and management academic, and holds the JC Penney professorship of management at MIT. He is best known for proposing the resource-based view of the firm in a 1984 journal article.

37. **Dean Wilde** is a strategy consultant and visiting professor of strategy at the MIT Sloan School of Management, who with Arnoldo Hax coauthored the book *The Delta Project: Discovering New Sources of Profitability in a Networked Economy*.

WORKS CITED

1. Aktouf, Omar, Miloud Chenoufi, and David Holford. "The False Expectations of Michael Porter's Strategic Management Framework." *Problems and Perspectives in Management* 4 (2005): 181–200.

2. Andrews, Kenneth R. *The Concept of Corporate Strategy.* Homewood, IL: R.D. Irwin, 1994.

3. Ankli, Robert E. "Michael Porter's Competitive Advantage and Business History." *Business and Economic History* 21 (1992): 228–36.

4. Argyres, Nicholas, and Anita McGahan. "An Interview with Michael Porter." *The Academy of Management Executive* 16.2 (May 2002): 43–52.

5. "Introduction: Michael Porter's *Competitive Strategy*." *The Academy of Management Executive* 16: 2 (May 2002): 41–42.

6. Bain, Joseph S. *Industrial Organization*. New York: John Wiley & Sons, Inc., 1959.

7. Barnard, Chester. *The Functions of the Executive*. Cambridge, MA: Harvard University Press, 1938.

8. Bedeian, Arthur, and Daniel Wren. "Most Influential Management Books of the 20th Century." *Organizational Dynamics* 29: 3 (Winter 2001): 221–25.

9. Brandenburger, Adam, and Barry Nalebuff. *Co-Opetition.* New York: Crown Business, 1996.

10. Bowman, Cliff. "Generic Strategies: A Substitute for Thinking?" *The Ashridge Journal* (2008): 1–28.

11. Broughton, Philip Delves. "Bogus Theories, Bad for Business." *Wall Street Journal*, August 5, 2009. Accessed January 24, 2016. http://www.wsj.com/articles/SB10001424052970204313604574329183846704634.

12. Chandler, Alfred. *The Visible Hand: The Managerial Revolution in American Business*. Cambridge, MA: Belknap Press, 1977.

13. *Strategy and Structure: Chapters in the History of the American Industrial Enterprise.* Cambridge, MA: MIT Press, 1962.

14. Chen, Yi-Gean. "The Relationship Between Competitive Strategies of

Kindergartens with Different Characteristics and Parent Satisfaction." *Journal of Global Business Management* 11.2 (2015): 76–87.

15. Colvin, Geoff. "There's No Quit in Michael Porter." *Fortune Magazine*, October 15, 2012. Accessed February 9, 2016. http://fortune.com/2012/10/15/theres-no-quit-in-michael-porter/.

16. Coyne, Kevin, and Somu Subramaniam. "Bringing Discipline to Strategy." *The McKinsey Quarterly* 4 (1996): 14–25.

17. Denning, Steve. "What Killed Michael Porter's Monitor Group? The One Force That Really Matters." *Forbes Magazine*, November 20, 2012. Accessed January 24, 2016. http://www.forbes.com/sites/stevedenning/2012/11/20/what-killed-michael-porters-monitor-group-the-one-force-that-really-matters/#d4b96f2733c7.

18. Dess, Gregory, Tom Lumpkin, Alan Eisner, and Gerry McNamara. *Strategic Management*. London: McGraw-Hill, 1995.

19. Downes, Larry. "Beyond Porter." *Context Magazine* December 1997.

20. Dulčić, Želimir, Vladimir Gnjidić, and Nikša Alfirević. "From Five Competitive Forces to Five Collaborative Forces: Revised View on Industry Structure-Firm Interrelationship." *Procedia—Social and Behavioral Sciences* 58 (2012): 1077–84.

21. *Economist, The,* editors. "Competitive Advantage." *The Economist*, August 4, 2008. Accessed February 8, 2016. www.economist.com/node/11869910.

22. "The Experience Curve." *The Economist*, September 14, 2009. Accessed February 8, 2016. http://www.economist.com/node/14298944.

23. Ford, Henry, with Samuel Crowther. *My Life and Work*. Garden City, NY: Doubleday, Page, 1923.

24. Fried, Vance, and Benjamin Oviatt. "Michael Porter's Missing Chapter: The Risk of Antitrust Violations." *The Academy of Management Executive*, 3.1 (1989): 49–56.

25. Gartner, William. "Review: *Competitive Strategy* and *Competitive Advantage*." *The Academy of Management Review* 10.4 (1985): 873–75.

26. Google Scholar. "Porter Competitive Strategy." Accessed on January 23, 2016. https://scholar.google.com/scholar?q=Porter+Competitive+Strategy&btnG=&hl=en&as_sdt=0%2C9.

27. "Porter Hypothesis." Accessed January 29, 2016. https://scholar.google.com/scholar?hl=en&q=%22Porter+Hypothesis%22&btnG=&as_sdt=1%2C9&as_sdtp=.

28. Hall, David, and Maurice Saias. "Strategy Follows Structure!" *Strategic Management Journal* 1.2 (1980): 149–63.

29. Hax, Arnoldo. *The Delta Model: Reinventing Your Business Strategy*. New York: Springer, 2009.

30. Indiatsy, Christopher, Muchero Mwangi, Evans Mandere, Julius Bichanga, and Gongera George. "The Application of Porter's Five Forces Model on Organization Performance: A Case of Cooperative Bank of Kenya Ltd." *European Journal of Business and Management* 6.16 (2014): 75–85.

31. Institute for Strategy and Competitiveness. "Home." Accessed January 29, 2016, http://www.isc.hbs.edu/.

32. Jelinek, Mariann. "Review of *The Competitive Advantage of Nations.*" *Administrative Science Quarterly* 37.3 (1992): 507–10.

33. Jörgensen, Ian. "Michael Porter's Contribution to Strategic Management." *Revista Base (Administração e Contabilidade) de UNISINOS* 5.3 (2008): 236–38.

34. Kiechel, Walter. *The Lords of Strategy: The Secret Intellectual History of the New Corporate World*. Cambridge, MA: Harvard Business Press, 2010.

35. Kim, Linsu, and Yooncheol Lim. "Environment, Generic Strategies, and Performance in a Rapidly Developing Country: A Taxonomic Approach." *The Academy of Management Journal* 31.4 (1998): 802–27.

36. Lawrence, Paul, and Jay Lorsch. *Organization and Environment*. Boston, MA: Harvard Business School, Division of Research,1967.

37. Learned, Philip, C. Roland Christensen, Kenneth R. Andrews, and William Guth. *Business Policy: Text and Cases*. Homewood, IL: R. D. Irwin, 1969.

38. Levitt, Theodore. "Marketing Myopia." *Harvard Business Review* (1960): 45–56.

39. Magretta, Joan. *Understanding Michael Porter: The Essential Guide to Competition and Strategy*. Cambridge, MA: Harvard Business Review Press, 2011.

40. Miller, Alex, and Gregory Dess. "Assessing Porter's (1980) Model in Terms of its Generalizability, Accuracy, and Simplicity." *Journal of Management Studies* 30 (1993): 553–85.

41. Mintzberg, Henry. "Generic Strategies: Toward a Comprehensive Framework." In *Advances in Strategic Management* vol. 5, edited by Robert Lamb and Paul Shrivastava, 1–67. Greenwich, CT: JAI Press, 1988.

42. Nieto-Rodriguez, Antonio. *The Focused Organization: How Concentrating on a Few Key Initiatives Can Dramatically Improve Strategy Execution*. Burlington, VT: Ashgate, 2012.

43. O'Shaughnessy, John. *Competitive Marketing: A Strategic Approach*. Boston, MA: Allen & Unwin, 1984.

44. Porter, Michael E. *Competitive Advantage: Creating and Sustaining Superior Performance*. New York: Free Press, 1985.

45. *The Competitive Advantage of Nations*. New York: Macmillan, 1990; 2nd ed., 1998.

46. *Competitive Strategy: Techniques for Analyzing Industries and Competitors*, 2nd ed. New York: Free Press, 1998.

47. "Curriculum Vitae." Accessed February 8, 2016. www.kozminski.edu.pl/uploads/import/kozminski/pl/default_opisy_2/3269/1/1/m._porter_-_kandydat_do_tytulu_doktora_honoris causa_alk.doc.

48. "How Competitive Forces Shape Strategy." *Harvard Business Review* 57.2 (1979): 86–93.

49. Porter, Michael E., and Mark R. Kramer. "Creating Shared Value." *Harvard Business Review* (2011): 63–70.

50. Porter, Michael E., Orjan Solvell, and I. Zander. *Advantage Sweden*. Stockholm: Norstedts Förlag, 1991.

51. Porter, Michael E., Hirotaka Takeuchi, and M. Sakakibara. *Can Japan Compete?* Basingstoke, UK: Macmillan Publishing, 2000.

52. Porter, Michael E., and Elizabeth O. Teisberg. *Redefining Health Care: Creating Value-Based Competition on Results.* Boston, MA: Harvard Business School Press, 2006.

53. Prajogo, Daniel I. "The Relationship Between Competitive Strategies and Product Quality." *Industrial Management & Data Systems* 107.1 (2007): 69–83.

54. Rivard, Suzanne, Louis Raymond, and David Verreault. "Resource-Based View and Competitive Strategy: An Integrated Model of the Contribution of Information Technology to Firm Performance." *The Journal of Strategic Information Systems* 15.1 (2006): 29–50.

55. Ryall, Michael. "The New Dynamics of Competition." *Harvard Business Review* (2013): 80–87.

56. Sasson, Amir. "Confining the Five Forces." *BI Strategy Magazine*, November 19, 2013. Accessed January 24, 2016. http://www.bi.edu/bizreview/articles/confining-the-five-forces-/.

57. Simon, Herbert. *Administrative Behavior: A Study of Decision-Making Processes in Administrative Organizations.* New York: Macmillan, 1947.

58. Slater, Stanley, and Thomas Zwirlein. "Shareholder Value and Investment Strategy Using the General Portfolio Model." *Journal of Management* 18.4 (1992): 717–32.

59. Spanos, Yiannis E., and Spyros Lioukas. "An Examination into the Causal Logic of Rent Generation: Contrasting Porter's Strategy Framework and the Resource-Based Perspective." *Strategic Management Journal* 22.10 (2001): 907–93.

60. Speed, Richard J. "Oh Mr Porter! A Re-Appraisal of Competitive Strategy." *Marketing Intelligence and Planning* 7.5/6 (1989): 8–11.

61. Stalk, George, Philip Evans, and Lawrence Shulman. "Competing on Capabilities: The New Rules of Corporate Strategy." *Harvard Business Review* 70.2 (1992): 57–69.

62. Stewart, Matthew. *The Management Myth: Debunking Modern Business Philosophy.* New York: W. W. Norton, 2009.

63. Taylor, Frederick Winslow. *The Principles of Scientific Management.* New York: Harper Brothers, 1911.

64. Wernerfelt, Birger. "A Resource-Based View of the Firm." *Strategic Management Journal* 5.2 (1984): 171–80.

65. Wright, Peter. "A Refinement of Porter's Strategies." *Strategic Management Journal* 8.1 (1987): 93–101.

66. Wright, Peter, Mark Kroll, Ben Kedia, and Charles Pringle. "Strategic Profiles, Market Share, and Business Performance." *Industrial Management* (1990): 23–28.

67. Yamamoto, Kan. "Kirin: Business Strategies for the Japanese Beer Market." MIT MBA Thesis at the Sloan School of Management, 2015.

原书作者简介

　　迈克尔·E. 波特 1947 年出生于美国一个军人家庭，从小辗转迁居多地。在中学和大学期间，波特擅长竞技体育项目，特别是棒球、橄榄球和高尔夫。他在普林斯顿大学主修航空航天和机械工程专业，1969 年以全班第一名的成绩毕业，随后在哈佛大学获得工商管理硕士和商业经济学博士学位。此后，他在哈佛商学院任教。从 2001 年起，波特任哈佛商学院战略与竞争力研究所主任。他是商业和经济学领域最知名的学者之一。

本书作者简介

　　帕德雷格·贝尔顿，牛津大学在读博士，专业方向为政治学和国际关系。他也是一位著作颇丰的新闻工作者，写作主题涵盖财经、商业和政治，作品主要发表于《爱尔兰时报》《卫报》《每日电讯报》《独立报》《爱尔兰独立报》《大西洋月刊》《新政治家》《远景》《泰晤士报文学副刊》《外交政策》等。

世界名著中的批判性思维

　　《世界思想宝库钥匙丛书》致力于深入浅出地阐释全世界著名思想家的观点，不论是谁、在何处都能了解到，从而推进批判性思维发展。

　　《世界思想宝库钥匙丛书》与世界顶尖大学的一流学者合作，为一系列学科中最有影响的著作推出新的分析文本，介绍其观点和影响。在这一不断扩展的系列中，每种选入的著作都代表了历经时间考验的思想典范。通过为这些著作提供必要背景、揭示原作者的学术渊源以及说明这些著作所产生的影响，本系列图书希望让读者以新视角看待这些划时代的经典之作。读者应学会思考、运用并挑战这些著作中的观点，而不是简单接受它们。

ABOUT THE AUTHOR OF THE ORIGINAL WORK

Michael E. Porter was born in 1947 into an American army family and lived in a number of different parts of the world while growing up. In secondary school and university he excelled in competitive sports, especially baseball, football, and golf. Porter earned an undergraduate degree in aerospace and mechanical engineering at Princeton University in 1969, graduating first in his class, and then went on to Harvard University for an MBA and a PhD in business economics. He then started lecturing at the Harvard Business School. Since 2001, Porter has directed Harvard's Institute for Strategy and Competitiveness. He is also one of the best-known academics in business and economics.

ABOUT THE AUTHOR OF THE ANALYSIS

Pádraig Belton undertook his doctoral research in politics and international relations at the University of Oxford. A prolific financial, business and political journalist, his work has appeared in publications including *The Irish Times, The Guardian, Telegraph, Independent, The Irish Independent, The Atlantic, The New Statesman, Prospect, The Times Literary Supplement*, and *Foreign Policy*.

ABOUT MACAT
GREAT WORKS FOR CRITICAL THINKING

Macat is focused on making the ideas of the world's great thinkers accessible and comprehensible to everybody, everywhere, in ways that promote the development of enhanced critical thinking skills.

It works with leading academics from the world's top universities to produce new analyses that focus on the ideas and the impact of the most influential works ever written across a wide variety of academic disciplines. Each of the works that sit at the heart of its growing library is an enduring example of great thinking. But by setting them in context — and looking at the influences that shaped their authors, as well as the responses they provoked — Macat encourages readers to look at these classics and game-changers with fresh eyes. Readers learn to think, engage and challenge their ideas, rather than simply accepting them.

批判性思维与《竞争战略：分析产业和竞争对手的技术》

首要批判性思维技巧：评估

次要批判性思维技巧：分析

迈克尔·E. 波特《竞争战略：分析产业和竞争对手的技术》（1980）是灵活运用批判性思维技巧的典范。波特用强有力的评估技巧，颠覆了商业界的很多思想传统。传统观点认为，公司要取得商业成功，最好的策略是全力扩大市场占有率；波特探讨了这种观点的利弊，对其可靠性提出了质疑。他认为扩大市场占有率并不是公司取得商业成功的唯一途径，并提供了有说服力的论据来证明这一点。他在著作中指明了产业的割裂性，即不同的公司服务于市场的不同部分（例如服装业存在低价大众市场和高价精品市场），并为企业在新兴市场、成熟市场和衰退市场中分别提供了战略。例如，印刷业属于衰退市场，但豪华工艺装订等高端产品仍有可观销路。

波特在《竞争战略》中也展示了其高超的分析技巧。他建议公司高管进行五力分析，五力是指五种竞争因素：新入市者、替代品、买方、供应商和业内竞争对手，它们一同塑造了公司的竞争环境。这一建议旨在界定这些看似不相干的竞争因素之间的关系，并促使读者检验其原有观点中隐含的假设。波特力避业内术语，行文直截了当，从而让读者更好地领略其评估的强大说服力。《竞争战略》对商业战略领域产生了深远的影响。

CRITICAL THINKING AND *COMPETITIVE STRATEGY*

• Primary critical thinking skill: EVALUATION
• Secondary critical thinking skill: ANALYSIS

Michael E. Porter's 1980 book *Competitive Strategy* is a fine example of critical thinking skills in action. Porter used his strong evaluative skills to overturn much of the accepted wisdom in the world of business. By exploring the strengths and weaknesses of the accepted argument that the best policy for firms to become more successful was to focus on expanding their market share, he was able to establish that the credibility of the argument was flawed. Porter did not believe such growth was the only way for a company to be successful, and provided compelling arguments as to why this was not the case. His book shows how industries can be fragmented, with different firms serving different parts of the market (the low-price mass market, and the expensive high-end market in clothing, for example) and examines strategies that businesses can follow in emerging, mature, and declining markets. If printing is in decline, for example, there may still be a market in this industry for high-end goods and services such as luxury craft bookbinding.

Porter also made excellent use of the critical thinking skill of analysis in writing *Competitive Strategy*. His advice that executives should analyze the five forces that mold the environment in which they compete — new entrants, substitute products, buyers, suppliers, and industry rivals — focused heavily on defining the relationships between these disparate factors and urged readers to check the assumptions of their arguments. Porter avoided technical jargon and wrote in a straightforward way to help readers see that his evaluation of the problem was strong. *Competitive Strategy* went on to be a highly influential work in the world of business strategy.

《世界思想宝库钥匙丛书》简介

《世界思想宝库钥匙丛书》致力于为一系列在各领域产生重大影响的人文社科类经典著作提供独特的学术探讨。每一本读物都不仅仅是原经典著作的内容摘要，而是介绍并深入研究原经典著作的学术渊源、主要观点和历史影响。这一丛书的目的是提供一套学习资料，以促进读者掌握批判性思维，从而更全面、深刻地去理解重要思想。

每一本读物分为 3 个部分：学术渊源、学术思想和学术影响，每个部分下有 4 个小节。这些章节旨在从各个方面研究原经典著作及其反响。

由于独特的体例，每一本读物不但易于阅读，而且另有一项优点：所有读物的编排体例相同，读者在进行某个知识层面的调查或研究时可交叉参阅多本该丛书中的相关读物，从而开启跨领域研究的路径。

为了方便阅读，每本读物最后还列出了术语表和人名表（在书中则以星号 * 标记），此外还有参考文献。

《世界思想宝库钥匙丛书》与剑桥大学合作，理清了批判性思维的要点，即如何通过 6 种技能来进行有效思考。其中 3 种技能让我们能够理解问题，另 3 种技能让我们有能力解决问题。这 6 种技能合称为"批判性思维 PACIER 模式"，它们是：

分析：了解如何建立一个观点；
评估：研究一个观点的优点和缺点；
阐释：对意义所产生的问题加以理解；
创造性思维：提出新的见解，发现新的联系；
解决问题：提出切实有效的解决办法；
理性化思维：创建有说服力的观点。

THE MACAT LIBRARY

The Macat Library is a series of unique academic explorations of seminal works in the humanities and social sciences — books and papers that have had a significant and widely recognised impact on their disciplines. It has been created to serve as much more than just a summary of what lies between the covers of a great book. It illuminates and explores the influences on, ideas of, and impact of that book. Our goal is to offer a learning resource that encourages critical thinking and fosters a better, deeper understanding of important ideas.

Each publication is divided into three Sections: Influences, Ideas, and Impact. Each Section has four Modules. These explore every important facet of the work, and the responses to it.

This Section-Module structure makes a Macat Library book easy to use, but it has another important feature. Because each Macat book is written to the same format, it is possible (and encouraged!) to cross-reference multiple Macat books along the same lines of inquiry or research. This allows the reader to open up interesting interdisciplinary pathways.

To further aid your reading, lists of glossary terms and people mentioned are included at the end of this book (these are indicated by an asterisk [*] throughout) — as well as a list of works cited.

Macat has worked with the University of Cambridge to identify the elements of critical thinking and understand the ways in which six different skills combine to enable effective thinking.

Three allow us to fully understand a problem; three more give us the tools to solve it. Together, these six skills make up the PACIER model of critical thinking. They are:

ANALYSIS — understanding how an argument is built
EVALUATION — exploring the strengths and weaknesses of an argument
INTERPRETATION — understanding issues of meaning
CREATIVE THINKING — coming up with new ideas and fresh connections
PROBLEM-SOLVING — producing strong solutions
REASONING — creating strong arguments

"《世界思想宝库钥匙丛书》提供了独一无二的跨学科学习和研究工具。它介绍那些革新了各自学科研究的经典著作，还邀请全世界一流专家和教育机构进行严谨的分析，为每位读者打开世界顶级教育的大门。"

—— 安德烈亚斯·施莱歇尔，
经济合作与发展组织教育与技能司司长

"《世界思想宝库钥匙丛书》直面大学教育的巨大挑战……他们组建了一支精干而活跃的学者队伍，来推出在研究广度上颇具新意的教学材料。"

—— 布罗尔斯教授、勋爵，剑桥大学前校长

"《世界思想宝库钥匙丛书》的愿景令人赞叹。它通过分析和阐释那些曾深刻影响人类思想以及社会、经济发展的经典文本，提供了新的学习方法。它推动批判性思维，这对于任何社会和经济体来说都是至关重要的。这就是未来的学习方法。"

—— 查尔斯·克拉克阁下，英国前教育大臣

"对于那些影响了各自领域的著作，《世界思想宝库钥匙丛书》能让人们立即了解到围绕那些著作展开的评论性言论，这让该系列图书成为在这些领域从事研究的师生们不可或缺的资源。"

—— 威廉·特朗佐教授，加利福尼亚大学圣地亚哥分校

"Macat offers an amazing first-of-its-kind tool for interdisciplinary learning and research. Its focus on works that transformed their disciplines and its rigorous approach, drawing on the world's leading experts and educational institutions, opens up a world-class education to anyone."

—— Andreas Schleicher, Director for Education and Skills, Organisation for Economic Co-operation and Development

"Macat is taking on some of the major challenges in university education... They have drawn together a strong team of active academics who are producing teaching materials that are novel in the breadth of their approach."

—— Prof Lord Broers, former Vice-Chancellor of the University of Cambridge

"The Macat vision is exceptionally exciting. It focuses upon new modes of learning which analyse and explain seminal texts which have profoundly influenced world thinking and so social and economic development. It promotes the kind of critical thinking which is essential for any society and economy. This is the learning of the future."

—— Rt Hon Charles Clarke, former UK Secretary of State for Education

"The Macat analyses provide immediate access to the critical conversation surrounding the books that have shaped their respective discipline, which will make them an invaluable resource to all of those, students and teachers, working in the field."

—— Prof William Tronzo, University of California at San Diego

The Macat Library
世界思想宝库钥匙丛书

TITLE	中文书名	类别
An Analysis of Arjun Appadurai's *Modernity at Large: Cultural Dimensions of Globalization*	解析阿尔君·阿帕杜莱《消失的现代性：全球化的文化维度》	人类学
An Analysis of Claude Lévi-Strauss's *Structural Anthropology*	解析克劳德·列维-斯特劳斯《结构人类学》	人类学
An Analysis of Marcel Mauss's *The Gift*	解析马塞尔·莫斯《礼物》	人类学
An Analysis of Jared M. Diamond's *Guns, Germs, and Steel: The Fate of Human Societies*	解析贾雷德·M.戴蒙德《枪炮、病菌与钢铁：人类社会的命运》	人类学
An Analysis of Clifford Geertz's *The Interpretation of Cultures*	解析克利福德·格尔茨《文化的解释》	人类学
An Analysis of Philippe Ariès's *Centuries of Childhood: A Social History of Family Life*	解析菲力浦·阿利埃斯《儿童的世纪：旧制度下的儿童和家庭生活》	人类学
An Analysis of W. Chan Kim & Renée Mauborgne's *Blue Ocean Strategy*	解析金伟灿/勒妮·莫博涅《蓝海战略》	商业
An Analysis of John P. Kotter's *Leading Change*	解析约翰·P.科特《领导变革》	商业
An Analysis of Michael E. Porter's *Competitive Strategy: Techniques for Analyzing Industries and Competitors*	解析迈克尔·E.波特《竞争战略：分析产业和竞争对手的技术》	商业
An Analysis of Jean Lave & Etienne Wenger's *Situated Learning: Legitimate Peripheral Participation*	解析琼·莱夫/艾蒂纳·温格《情境学习：合法的边缘性参与》	商业
An Analysis of Douglas McGregor's *The Human Side of Enterprise*	解析道格拉斯·麦格雷戈《企业的人性面》	商业
An Analysis of Milton Friedman's *Capitalism and Freedom*	解析米尔顿·弗里德曼《资本主义与自由》	商业
An Analysis of Ludwig von Mises's *The Theory of Money and Credit*	解析路德维希·冯·米塞斯《货币和信用理论》	经济学
An Analysis of Adam Smith's *The Wealth of Nations*	解析亚当·斯密《国富论》	经济学
An Analysis of Thomas Piketty's *Capital in the Twenty-First Century*	解析托马斯·皮凯蒂《21世纪资本论》	经济学
An Analysis of Nassim Nicholas Taleb's *The Black Swan: The Impact of the Highly Improbable*	解析纳西姆·尼古拉斯·塔勒布《黑天鹅：如何应对不可预知的未来》	经济学
An Analysis of Ha-Joon Chang's *Kicking Away the Ladder*	解析张夏准《富国陷阱：发达国家为何踢开梯子》	经济学
An Analysis of Thomas Robert Malthus's *An Essay on the Principle of Population*	解析托马斯·罗伯特·马尔萨斯《人口论》	经济学

An Analysis of John Maynard Keynes's *The General Theory of Employment, Interest and Money*	解析约翰·梅纳德·凯恩斯《就业、利息和货币通论》	经济学
An Analysis of Milton Friedman's *The Role of Monetary Policy*	解析米尔顿·弗里德曼《货币政策的作用》	经济学
An Analysis of Burton G. Malkiel's *A Random Walk Down Wall Street*	解析伯顿·G.马尔基尔《漫步华尔街》	经济学
An Analysis of Friedrich A. Hayek's *The Road to Serfdom*	解析弗里德里希·A.哈耶克《通往奴役之路》	经济学
An Analysis of Charles P. Kindleberger's *Manias, Panics, and Crashes: A History of Financial Crises*	解析查尔斯·P.金德尔伯格《疯狂、惊恐和崩溃：金融危机史》	经济学
An Analysis of Amartya Sen's *Development as Freedom*	解析阿马蒂亚·森《以自由看待发展》	经济学
An Analysis of Rachel Carson's *Silent Spring*	解析蕾切尔·卡森《寂静的春天》	地理学
An Analysis of Charles Darwin's *On the Origin of Species: by Means of Natural Selection, or The Preservation of Favoured Races in the Struggle for Life*	解析查尔斯·达尔文《物种起源》	地理学
An Analysis of World Commission on Environment and Development's *The Brundtland Report: Our Common Future*	解析世界环境与发展委员会《布伦特兰报告：我们共同的未来》	地理学
An Analysis of James E. Lovelock's *Gaia: A New Look at Life on Earth*	解析詹姆斯·E.拉伍洛克《盖娅：地球生命的新视野》	地理学
An Analysis of Paul Kennedy's *The Rise and Fall of the Great Powers: Economic Change and Military Conflict from 1500–2000*	解析保罗·肯尼迪《大国的兴衰：1500—2000年的经济变革与军事冲突》	历史
An Analysis of Janet L. Abu-Lughod's *Before European Hegemony: The World System A. D. 1250–1350*	解析珍妮特·L.阿布-卢格霍德《欧洲霸权之前：1250—1350年的世界体系》	历史
An Analysis of Alfred W. Crosby's *The Columbian Exchange: Biological and Cultural Consequences of 1492*	解析艾尔弗雷德·W.克罗斯比《哥伦布大交换：1492年以后的生物影响和文化冲击》	历史
An Analysis of Tony Judt's *Postwar: A History of Europe since 1945*	解析托尼·朱特《战后欧洲史》	历史
An Analysis of Richard J. Evans's *In Defence of History*	解析理查德·J.艾文斯《捍卫历史》	历史
An Analysis of Eric Hobsbawm's *The Age of Revolution: Europe 1789–1848*	解析艾瑞克·霍布斯鲍姆《革命的年代：欧洲1789—1848年》	历史

An Analysis of Roland Barthes's *Mythologies*	解析罗兰·巴特《神话学》	文学与批判理论
An Analysis of Simone de Beauvoir's *The Second Sex*	解析西蒙娜·德·波伏娃《第二性》	文学与批判理论
An Analysis of Edward W. Said's *Orientalism*	解析爱德华·W. 萨义德《东方主义》	文学与批判理论
An Analysis of Virginia Woolf's *A Room of One's Own*	解析弗吉尼亚·伍尔芙《一间自己的房间》	文学与批判理论
An Analysis of Judith Butler's *Gender Trouble*	解析朱迪斯·巴特勒《性别麻烦》	文学与批判理论
An Analysis of Ferdinand de Saussure's *Course in General Linguistics*	解析费尔迪南·德·索绪尔《普通语言学教程》	文学与批判理论
An Analysis of Susan Sontag's *On Photography*	解析苏珊·桑塔格《论摄影》	文学与批判理论
An Analysis of Walter Benjamin's *The Work of Art in the Age of Mechanical Reproduction*	解析瓦尔特·本雅明《机械复制时代的艺术作品》	文学与批判理论
An Analysis of W. E. B. Du Bois's *The Souls of Black Folk*	解析W.E.B. 杜波依斯《黑人的灵魂》	文学与批判理论
An Analysis of Plato's *The Republic*	解析柏拉图《理想国》	哲学
An Analysis of Plato's *Symposium*	解析柏拉图《会饮篇》	哲学
An Analysis of Aristotle's *Metaphysics*	解析亚里士多德《形而上学》	哲学
An Analysis of Aristotle's *Nicomachean Ethics*	解析亚里士多德《尼各马可伦理学》	哲学
An Analysis of Immanuel Kant's *Critique of Pure Reason*	解析伊曼努尔·康德《纯粹理性批判》	哲学
An Analysis of Ludwig Wittgenstein's *Philosophical Investigations*	解析路德维希·维特根斯坦《哲学研究》	哲学
An Analysis of G. W. F. Hegel's *Phenomenology of Spirit*	解析 G. W. F. 黑格尔《精神现象学》	哲学
An Analysis of Baruch Spinoza's *Ethics*	解析巴鲁赫·斯宾诺莎《伦理学》	哲学
An Analysis of Hannah Arendt's *The Human Condition*	解析汉娜·阿伦特《人的境况》	哲学
An Analysis of G. E. M. Anscombe's *Modern Moral Philosophy*	解析 G. E. M. 安斯康姆《现代道德哲学》	哲学
An Analysis of David Hume's *An Enquiry Concerning Human Understanding*	解析大卫·休谟《人类理解研究》	哲学

An Analysis of Søren Kierkegaard's *Fear and Trembling*	解析索伦·克尔凯郭尔《恐惧与战栗》	哲学
An Analysis of René Descartes's *Meditations on First Philosophy*	解析勒内·笛卡尔《第一哲学沉思录》	哲学
An Analysis of Friedrich Nietzsche's *On the Genealogy of Morality*	解析弗里德里希·尼采《论道德的谱系》	哲学
An Analysis of Gilbert Ryle's *The Concept of Mind*	解析吉尔伯特·赖尔《心的概念》	哲学
An Analysis of Thomas Kuhn's *The Structure of Scientific Revolutions*	解析托马斯·库恩《科学革命的结构》	哲学
An Analysis of John Stuart Mill's *Utilitarianism*	解析约翰·斯图亚特·穆勒《功利主义》	哲学
An Analysis of Aristotle's *Politics*	解析亚里士多德《政治学》	政治学
An Analysis of Niccolò Machiavelli's *The Prince*	解析尼科洛·马基雅维利《君主论》	政治学
An Analysis of Karl Marx's *Capital*	解析卡尔·马克思《资本论》	政治学
An Analysis of Benedict Anderson's *Imagined Communities*	解析本尼迪克特·安德森《想象的共同体》	政治学
An Analysis of Samuel P. Huntington's *The Clash of Civilizations and the Remaking of World Order*	解析塞缪尔·P.亨廷顿《文明的冲突与世界秩序的重建》	政治学
An Analysis of Alexis de Tocqueville's *Democracy in America*	解析阿列克西·德·托克维尔《论美国的民主》	政治学
An Analysis of John A. Hobson's *Imperialism: A Study*	解析约翰·A.霍布森《帝国主义》	政治学
An Analysis of Thomas Paine's *Common Sense*	解析托马斯·潘恩《常识》	政治学
An Analysis of John Rawls's *A Theory of Justice*	解析约翰·罗尔斯《正义论》	政治学
An Analysis of Francis Fukuyama's *The End of History and the Last Man*	解析弗朗西斯·福山《历史的终结与最后的人》	政治学
An Analysis of John Locke's *Two Treatises of Government*	解析约翰·洛克《政府论》	政治学
An Analysis of Sun Tzu's *The Art of War*	解析孙武《孙子兵法》	政治学
An Analysis of Henry Kissinger's *World Order: Reflections on the Character of Nations and the Course of History*	解析亨利·基辛格《世界秩序》	政治学
An Analysis of Jean-Jacques Rousseau's *The Social Contract*	解析让-雅克·卢梭《社会契约论》	政治学

An Analysis of Odd Arne Westad's *The Global Cold War: Third World Interventions and the Making of Our Times*	解析文安立《全球冷战：美苏对第三世界的干涉与当代世界的形成》	政治学
An Analysis of Sigmund Freud's *The Interpretation of Dreams*	解析西格蒙德·弗洛伊德《梦的解析》	心理学
An Analysis of William James' *The Principles of Psychology*	解析威廉·詹姆斯《心理学原理》	心理学
An Analysis of Philip Zimbardo's *The Lucifer Effect*	解析菲利普·津巴多《路西法效应》	心理学
An Analysis of Leon Festinger's *A Theory of Cognitive Dissonance*	解析利昂·费斯汀格《认知失调论》	心理学
An Analysis of Richard H. Thaler & Cass R. Sunstein's *Nudge: Improving Decisions about Health, Wealth, and Happiness*	解析理查德·H.泰勒／卡斯·R.桑斯坦《助推：如何做出有关健康、财富和幸福的更优决策》	心理学
An Analysis of Gordon Allport's *The Nature of Prejudice*	解析高尔登·奥尔波特《偏见的本质》	心理学
An Analysis of Steven Pinker's *The Better Angels of Our Nature: Why Violence Has Declined*	解析斯蒂芬·平克《人性中的善良天使：暴力为什么会减少》	心理学
An Analysis of Stanley Milgram's *Obedience to Authority*	解析斯坦利·米尔格拉姆《对权威的服从》	心理学
An Analysis of Betty Friedan's *The Feminine Mystique*	解析贝蒂·弗里丹《女性的奥秘》	心理学
An Analysis of David Riesman's *The Lonely Crowd: A Study of the Changing American Character*	解析大卫·理斯曼《孤独的人群：美国人社会性格演变之研究》	社会学
An Analysis of Franz Boas's *Race, Language and Culture*	解析弗朗兹·博厄斯《种族、语言与文化》	社会学
An Analysis of Pierre Bourdieu's *Outline of a Theory of Practice*	解析皮埃尔·布尔迪厄《实践理论大纲》	社会学
An Analysis of Max Weber's *The Protestant Ethic and the Spirit of Capitalism*	解析马克斯·韦伯《新教伦理与资本主义精神》	社会学
An Analysis of Jane Jacobs's *The Death and Life of Great American Cities*	解析简·雅各布斯《美国大城市的死与生》	社会学
An Analysis of C. Wright Mills's *The Sociological Imagination*	解析C.赖特·米尔斯《社会学的想象力》	社会学
An Analysis of Robert E. Lucas Jr.'s *Why Doesn't Capital Flow from Rich to Poor Countries?*	解析小罗伯特·E.卢卡斯《为何资本不从富国流向穷国？》	社会学

An Analysis of Émile Durkheim's *On Suicide*	解析埃米尔·迪尔凯姆《自杀论》	社会学
An Analysis of Eric Hoffer's *The True Believer: Thoughts on the Nature of Mass Movements*	解析埃里克·霍弗《狂热分子：群众运动圣经》	社会学
An Analysis of Jared M. Diamond's *Collapse: How Societies Choose to Fail or Survive*	解析贾雷德·M.戴蒙德《大崩溃：社会如何选择兴亡》	社会学
An Analysis of Michel Foucault's *The History of Sexuality Vol. 1: The Will to Knowledge*	解析米歇尔·福柯《性史（第一卷）：求知意志》	社会学
An Analysis of Michel Foucault's *Discipline and Punish*	解析米歇尔·福柯《规训与惩罚》	社会学
An Analysis of Richard Dawkins's *The Selfish Gene*	解析理查德·道金斯《自私的基因》	社会学
An Analysis of Antonio Gramsci's *Prison Notebooks*	解析安东尼奥·葛兰西《狱中札记》	社会学
An Analysis of Augustine's *Confessions*	解析奥古斯丁《忏悔录》	神学
An Analysis of C. S. Lewis's *The Abolition of Man*	解析 C. S. 路易斯《人之废》	神学

图书在版编目（CIP）数据

解析迈克尔·E. 波特《竞争战略：分析产业和竞争对手的技术》: 汉、英 /
帕德雷格·贝尔顿（Pádraig Belton）著；陶庆译 . —上海：上海外语教
育出版社，2020
（世界思想宝库钥匙丛书）
ISBN 978-7-5446-6447-9

I.①解… Ⅱ.①帕… ②陶… Ⅲ.①竞争战略－研究－汉、英 Ⅳ.①F110

中国版本图书馆CIP数据核字（2020）第079927号

This Chinese-English bilingual edition of *An Analysis of Michael E. Porter's* Competitive
Strategy: Techniques for Analyzing Industries and Competitors is published by arrangement with
Macat International Limited.
Licensed for sale throughout the world.

本书汉英双语版由Macat国际有限公司授权上海外语教育出版社有限公司出版。
供在全世界范围内发行、销售。

图字：09 - 2018 - 549

出版发行：上海外语教育出版社
　　　　　　（上海外国语大学内）　邮编：200083
电　　　话：021-65425300（总机）
电子邮箱：bookinfo@sflep.com.cn
网　　　址：http://www.sflep.com
责任编辑：梁瀚杰

印　　　刷：上海信老印刷厂
开　　　本：890×1240　1/32　印张 6.875　字数 142千字
版　　　次：2020 年 9月第 1版　　2020 年 9月第 1次印刷
印　　　数：2 100 册

书　　　号：ISBN 978-7-5446-6447-9
定　　　价：30.00 元
　　　本版图书如有印装质量问题，可向本社调换
　　　质量服务热线：4008-213-263　电子邮箱：editorial@sflep.com